Gimme 15 Inches

Rants, raves and deadline-driven observations

Dave Molter

Illustrations by Michael J. Andrulonis

Handbasket Books
www.handbasketbooks.com

Acknowledgment is made to the Washington (Pa.) *Observer-Reporter* newspaper, in which these columns first appeared, some with different titles and in different form; and to *Dead Center Magazine*, in which "In My Life: How the Beatles Saved Me, and Everyone" first appeared in 2014.

"A Child's Garden of Curses" and "Childhood's End" appear in print for the first time.

Cover design and illustrations by Michael J. Andrulonis: www.andrudesign.com

ISBN: 0-692-85557-2
ISBN-13: 978-0-692-85557-7

For Pam, my soulmate, who rescued me in so many ways.
Straight down the line, baby.

Contents

Acknowledgments

Many have supported, encouraged and prodded me in my writing endeavors since I first sat down at my sister Pat's portable typewriter at age 10. Kudos and thanks to:

Angie Mullig, my editor, a talented writer and my closest friend since we labored together at the University of Pittsburgh Medical Center PR gulag in 1992. My proofreader and sounding board since I began writing columns again, Angie not only transcribed some of my older columns (I am a lousy typist) but also devised categories and wrote their introductions. A kindred spirit, Angie has a warped sense of humor that at times exceeds my own. When needed—as in my long-delayed production of this book—she serves as cadence beater to my reluctant galley slave. She also has the guts to tell me when something I write sucks. For this she earns my love and respect.

Michael J. Andrulonis, whose inspired cover art and illustrations far exceed my proletariat vision.

The late **Byron Smialek**, who as news editor of the Washington

(Pa.) *Observer-Reporter* read the suburban weekly clips I provided at my interview, but hired me anyway. Byron allowed me unprecedented latitude in subject matter as a columnist and seldom changed a word, even when he knew readers would not understand and react negatively. Byron also told me—whispering to me from behind his desk, which abutted mine—the funniest legless-Mexican-hooker joke I have ever heard. Maybe in my next book.

Brant Newman, writer, editor and current assistant editor of the O-R, who in 2010 suggested me when the paper needed a new columnist. Like Byron, Brant allows me a free hand in subject matter, editing only to avoid misspelling or slander. This earns him— even though he is an atheist—a spot hawking hot dogs in Hell with me in the afterlife.

Park Burroughs, first for listening when Brant recommended me and for, many years previously, explaining how to get a bad word into a "family newspaper." It played thusly: I used the word "crap" in a column. Park, proofing it, said, "You can't say crap! Everyone knows you mean shit!" A week later, Park used "sucks" in his column. Why, I inquired, was he allowed to do so? "Because it was a direct quote!" he said. "So," I reasoned, "I could have used 'shit' if I had used it in a direct quote?" His exasperated sigh perfectly summed up the editor-writer relationship.

Steve Molter, my son, who after never writing more than two paragraphs for any high school assignment laid a 250,000-word fantasy manuscript on me at age 19, spurring me to think I might do the same.

Steve Allen, Ernie Kovacs, Mel Brooks, Carl Reiner, Sid Caesar and the raft of comics I grew up watching on TV as well as to the staff writers at *Mad* magazine. Their quirky sense of humor and wordplay helped mold mine. Ain't no such thing as a bad pun.

Foreword

My apologies to anyone who, based on its title, bought this book expecting a memoir of my years in the porn industry. Silly! If that were so, it would be a hardcover.

"Gimme 15 Inches" is a variation of what newspaper editors say to reporters who arrive back at the office after an assignment, at deadline, ready to write. Editors create page layouts in advance, leaving a certain number of "column inches" blank. This they charmingly call the "news hole." Reporters fill that hole.

Hmmm. That *does* sound pornographic!

But it's an apt description. Each column herein takes up about 15 inches of space in the Washington (Pa.) *Observer-Reporter* newspaper, where they began appearing in 1989 after I was hired as a beat reporter. It was my first real writing job. Beat reporters most often cover police news, local government and schools; they occasionally may write a longer "feature" story. But our news editor also encouraged us to write columns—a.k.a., opinion pieces—once a month. Some of my colleagues shied from the task, but I relished it. My editor liked my style, and soon I was writing a column every week.

I left the O-R in 1992 but returned when the atmosphere at the public relations writing job I'd taken became anal-retentive. I left permanently in 1994, and my column writing ceased until 2010. That's when the O-R's then-managing editor asked if I would be interested in returning as a freelancer. I jumped at the chance.

Many will find my columns goofy, implausible or snide. That's fine. I began writing for my own amusement, and that's still my approach. I am continually baffled when readers take offense at what I consider to be innocuous things; I am equally surprised when a column I think is a throwaway elicits praise. Quite often I write a piece making fun of both sides of an issue. When someone from each side thanks me, I know I have succeeded in my real goal—sowing confusion in the already weed-choked gardens of readers' minds.

This book is arranged in sections of like subject matter, but columns needn't be read in order or in sections. I have provided historical context to clarify references that were topical at the time of the column's original publication but which may seem quizzical today.

Read on! You know you want it!

It's Refreshing!

WARNING: CONSUMPTION MAY CAUSE DIZZINESS, SHORTNESS OF BREATH, PALPITATIONS, FACIAL TICS, MAN-BOOBS, HAIRY PALMS, EXPLOSIVE DIARRHEA, HOOF-IN-MOUTH DISEASE AND DEATH...ENJOY!

Consumerism: The Final Frontier

Dave is not your typical consumer. The man's house is a salute to the 1950s, with plastic stained-glass room dividers—except the parts of the house that serve as shrines to the Beatles. His bottle opener collection includes one vaguely obscene gadget with a nude female torso that serves as a handle, a bigmouthed, near-perfect depiction of Donald Trump and one decidedly irreverent Christ the Redeemer "church key." His fashion sense is unapologetically retro. Paisley shirts? Certainly. Pointy-toed purple paisley shoes? *Natürlich*. Rakishly tilted berets? *Mais oui!* So it's no surprise that Dave has a skewed perspective of what good old-fashioned American consumerism should be. From the iconic G.I. Joe to post-apocalypse zombie defense kits, Dave takes on capitalism, marketing tactics, international import laws and the appalling gullibility of consumers. But he's a fair man who would probably argue that your purchase of this book demonstrates that you're willing to invest in goods of questionable value. It's too late now. You bought this book, so you might as well read the essays that follow.

G.I. Blues

Author's note: This column first appeared in 1989.

The news broke Thursday, and it was not pleasant. Across America, and possibly around the world, millions of husbands and fathers had their manhood snatched away from them by the U.S. judicial system. So terrible was the decision handed down by the U.S. Court of Appeals for the District of Columbia that I hesitate to repeat it. But, for those dads who remain unaware, here it is.

G.I. Joe, with whom so many fathers and sons have spent weekend afternoons crawling on their bellies through the weeds, is not a toy soldier. He is a ... maybe I'd better spell it: D-O-L-L.

First, they stop the draft. Then they tell us, "Go ahead: Burn the flag." Now this. All along, maybe the Marines should've been looking for a few good mannequins.

A D _ _ _? The decision is treasonous! Don't try to camouflage it.

Hasbro Industries Inc., which began manufacturing Joe in 1964, appealed an earlier, similar anti-G.I. ruling by the U.S. Customs Department. Hasbro maintained its proto-Rambo is merely an updated version of the toy soldier. By doing so, they hoped to avoid a 12-percent import tariff the Customs Service imposes on ... that word ... but not on replications of trained military personnel.

Import tariff? Wait a minute. They don't mean ...?

Sorry, but they do. Since 1982, Joe has come from Hong Kong. Not only is Joe a, you know, but the All-American fighting man is an immigrant. Is nothing sacred? But, like the captain of the Titanic and the iceberg, we should've seen this coming.

The first clue came back in 1976, when Joe went from an imposing 11½-inch military giant down to an 8½-inch grunt. Then, in 1982, after sweating out the anti-war movement, Joe shrank again, to a piddling 3½ inches. Next, they replaced his removable khakis with permanently painted-on fatigues — the guy can't even change his underwear anymore. No wonder they tell us the Russkies can kick the New Army's collective butt. All that was bad enough.

But now, they want to drive Joe to his flexible-plastic, bendable knees by saying he's a ... thing girls play with. Has the Veterans Administration heard about this?

This whole business confused me, so I decided to check with an expert: my 5-year-old nephew.

"Hey," I said as he played with his "Ghostbusters" ectoplasm in a can, "They say G.I. Joe's a doll, not a soldier. How do you feel about that?"

"N-o-o-o-o-o," he said, half giggling, as if I'd told him eggs come from chickens, not the grocery store. "He's a guy. Jessica (his sister) plays with dolls. Not me. Not boys."

The kid is obviously Green Beret material.

G.I. Joe not a toy soldier? Next, they'll say the Transformers aren't really beings from another planet. A doll?

Say it ain't so, Joe.

Ken Comes of Age

Author's note: Readers needn't be worried that every column in this collection is about dolls, although I have written about Barbie and her pals far more than I would like to admit.

Proof that I am out of the loop came last week when I realized that I had missed the arrival of the 2014 *Sports Illustrated* swimsuit edition on newsstands. I wasn't surprised: The sight of lithesome young women writhing on the beach while wearing what appears to be three Post-It notes held in place by dental floss stopped titillating me around 1960. That was the year I began "borrowing" my brother's *Playboy* magazines. Too much, too soon.

These days it's the mystery that excites me: a woman's well-turned ankle peeking out below the hem of an evening gown; a clinging cashmere sweater. But what drew my attention to the current swimsuit edition is the furor over the appearance of leggy supermodel Barbie on an "ad overwrap" that makes it appear as if she is the cover girl.

The overwrap appeared on only 1,000 of the nearly 6 million copies the issue was projected to sell. But it was savvy marketing by Mattel, Barbie's manufacturer, which is distributing a Sports Illustrated Swimsuit Edition Barbie that retails for $29.95. Little girls are not SI's target market, but Mattel likely anticipated the upheaval—and press coverage—the cover caused.

Now, some might argue that SI's swimsuit issue is already filled with plastic women, so why raise a stink over the addition of one more? But to feminists—perhaps a word that anyone younger than 30 will have to look up—Barbie and her impossibly sculpted body perpetuate stereotypes. This is not a new observation.

Complaints began almost immediately after Barbie first appeared in 1959. Even in that "Mad Men" era of rampant female objectification, woman quickly noticed that there was something fishy about Barbie's measurements. Barbie stands 11.5 inches tall and measures 5.5-2.75-5.25. Using the Secret Barbie Multiplier of 6.55, I have determined that in the real world these figures translate to 5 feet, 9 inches tall and 36-18-34.

Never mind how I arrived at these figures. Let's just say that the image of a grown man hunched over a Barbie doll, a cloth tape measure in hand, is not one I want to appear on my Facebook page.

These are not unrealistic measurements, but they are seldom achieved in real life. Yes, it's true that I once dated a woman who had an 18-inch waist. Yes, she was slim and blonde, had closetsful of clothes and walked on her toes most of the time. Yes, she left me for a guy named Ken. Art imitating life, or vice versa? A question for the ages.

Despite this proof—and Mattel's attempts over the years to make Barbie a role model for girls by introducing Astronaut Barbie, Veterinarian Barbie, Gulf War-era Army Barbie and even Episcopal Priest Barbie—women remain upset. I understand. Because I hate Ken.

Barbie's boyfriend appeared in 1961, yet has been impervious to the ravages of time. Really, when did you last run across a real

63-year-old man who looks like Ken—disgustingly ripped and dressed in the latest fashions? Yet Ken is still being foisted upon men as a role model. It's time we get real. Ken 2014 should reflect the true state of most 63-year-old males:

Introducing **Beer Gut Ken.** *An understated "Git–R-Done" baseball cap first draws your attention and leads your eyes naturally downward past an eight-day growth of beard to a faded red-and-black plaid flannel shirt tucked into and spilling over the elasticized waistband of faded denim boot-cut jeans, which break over the top of immaculate white New Balance cross trainers. Accessories include "Just for Ken" hair dye, a tiny tube of testosterone-boosting cream and, in the Dream House medicine chest, an itty-bitty bottle of Barbi-turates to help him cope with the success of his plastic paramour.*

The bottle's safety cap is off because Ken's non-articulated arthritic fingers don't work so well anymore.

Bob-Bob-Bobbleheadin' Along

Author's note: This column first appeared in 2012.

The flap created by the recent marketing of a bobblehead doll in the likeness of presidential assassin John Wilkes Booth qualifies as Ford's Theatre of the Absurd.

The Associated Press reported March 16 that the Gettysburg Museum and Visitor Center had lowered the curtain on sales of the Derringer-toting Booth replica—this after a reporter for the Hanover (Pa.) *Evening Star* ran a story questioning the doll's appropriateness. Before the story broke nationally, a little more than half the initial run of 250 dolls marketed online and in stores by BobbleHead, LLC had been sold. Now, thanks to the publicity, they're selling even faster, and more have been ordered for production. Twenty bucks will get you Booth-in-a-Box—a box that replicates the interior of Ford's Theatre, where Booth assassinated our 16th president in 1865.

A spokesman for BobbleHead, LLC, told reporter Tim Prudente, "We make [the Booth bobblehead] for people that are into Civil

War memorabilia. It's supposed to be a gag gift." And gag some did. But I'm not sure why.

My initial thought after reading about the Booth doll was, "I guess this means the Lego Grassy Knoll set is canceled." But, then, I had also thought that an exploding space shuttle would sell pretty well after the Challenger disaster. After all, joking is part of the catharsis that trails a tragedy. And it's not like we're consistent in defining what offends us.

I heard jokes about the Challenger explosion about a week after it occurred in 1986; I heard a joke about 9/11 on 9/12. (They took away an old lady's knitting needles on a plane because she said she was making an Afghan.)

Robert E. Lee was responsible for the death of a lot more Northerners than was Booth, yet his bobblehead doll is still being sold. Ditto Ulysses S. Grant, who offed a lot of graycoats. And I imagine there are some who are still miffed that Lincoln freed the slaves. But are they pulling bobblehead Abe off the shelf? Besides, during the celebration of the centennial of the Civil War in the 1960s, Hasbro successfully marketed a Johnny Reb cannon. So what's the problem with John Wilkes Bobblehead?

In the mid-1960s, about the same time as the publication of "Unsafe at Any Speed," Ralph Nader's indictment of the auto industry, Tri-Play Toys made a bundle selling the Crashmobile, a toy car that flew to pieces when it hit an obstacle (thus predating my exploding Challenger idea). Yet General Motors didn't try to have it removed from shelves.

And it's not like other infamous men and even sacred cows don't have their tiny heads stuck on a spring and attached to a tiny body. Bobbleheads of Osama Bin Laden, Fidel Castro, Jesus, Moses and even of scientist Marie Curie, which glows in the dark (she pioneered research into radioactivity), remain on the market. So really, who decides what's offensive?

You do. Here's an opportunity.

The anglicized face of Jesus appears on a serving tray, staring off into the distance as if checking out the menu at Starbucks and inviting stains to rival those on the Shroud of Turin. And there once was a Jesus Pez dispenser. Sacrilegious? A crocheted comforter bears the likenesses of John F. Kennedy, Robert F. Kennedy and Martin Luther King Jr. A fitting tribute to their memory?

Is plastic vomit funny? OK … your daughter's bulimic. Is it funny now? How about video of people falling off trampolines and men being hit in the testicles? Funny? Not to me. But if they're not, then why is "America's Funniest Home Videos" so popular? It's all relative.

Yeah, I know. About all you can do is shake your head.

Potty On, People!

A bit more than a decade ago, I accompanied several colleagues on a business trip to the Philippines to attend a conference, the purpose of which, ostensibly, was to deal with the worsening vehicle-produced air pollution in that nation's capital city, Manila.

About 1,000 auto executives, engineers, scientists and writers descended on Manila, met for three days, took a day to ruminate, then presented findings to anxious Filipinos before noon on Friday, when the visitors' planes were scheduled to depart. Their conclusion: Manila's air was polluted.

"We know that," Filipino officials said, with some exasperation. "How can we fix it?"

"We're here to tell you what's wrong," the fact-finders replied, "not how to fix it." Then they flew home.

Through this modern fable we see that even highly educated, experienced, well-intentioned engineers fail. As have those who invented the Numi toilet from Kohler, a technojohn that—with its $6,390 price tag—redefines the meaning of human waste.

I'm not against innovation in plumbing. Padded seats? Wonderful! Autoflushing in public restrooms? Long overdue! But really ... I don't think that when Handel wrote "Water Music," he had in mind a toilet that has a jack for your iPod and built-in speakers. Numi has these, and more. Such as:

- A lid and seat that open automatically when motion is detected at the front of the unit (Not great if you struggle to keep your dog from drinking out of the toilet, but ...)
- Ambient lighting from its posterior portion (it's tankless)
- A heated seat
- A footwarmer
- A built-in deodorizer
- A bidet function
- Heated, adjustable, forced-air drying
- Autoflushing
- A remote control

A remote control?

Yes, the Numi comes with an iPhone-like, touchpad wireless remote that allows up to five users to store favorite settings. So, if you prefer your bathroom break to include a heated seat and feet, plus music by Prince ("Tonight I'm gonna potty like it's 1999 ..."), Numi can provide that combo. Let's not speculate on what kind of pictures might result if a Numi user confuses his crapper zapper with his iPhone.

There's little doubt that Numi is a technological wonder. It's sleek. It's stylish. But does it address the question that surely must be on every female reader's mind: Does Numi solve the age-old problem of MFRLS—Male Failure to Raise and Lower Seat?

Kinda.

A video on the Kohler Web site shows Numi magically opening and closing both lid and seat automatically. But neither the video nor the accompanying text explains if the lid can be opened separately, leaving the seat down. However, that must be the case. In an interview with the *New York Times*, company President David Kohler explains that Numi allows a man to place a foot near a special sensor to raise the seat separately.

You have to use your foot? A $6,400 commode that can't sense the user's gender? Like they say, they can put a man on the moon, but …

I'm sorry ladies. Numi still requires action and awareness on the part of male users. But at least it doesn't require a man to bend over, lift the seat by hand, lower it by hand, close the lid and flush by hand … all in time to get back to the game before the commercial is over. That's a start.

I'm here to tell you what's wrong, not how to fix it.

Fork It Over

Hurry, hurry! Step right up! Folks, you say you're having trouble sticking to your New Year's resolution to eat less. You say you want to lose weight, but you just can't stop your arm from shoveling food into your mouth faster than the fireman throwing coal into the boiler of a steam locomotive trying to outrun an Apache war party!

Well, folks, I'm here to tell you not to lose hope. Because I have a simple, four-word solution to all your eating woes. And those words are, "Tech. Nol. O. Gee." You heard me right, ma'am.

Folks, take a gander at HAPIfork, an electronic eating utensil that warns you when you're eating too fast. How? I'm gonna tell ya how, mister!

You program HAPIfork using an application for your smart-phone or computer—you have a smartphone, don't ya, kid?—and here's how it works. Now, I'm no rocket scientist, folks, so I'm gonna read from this here piece of paper provided by HAPIlabs, HAPIfork's inventors, who may be rocket scientists but, even if they aren't, at least know how to spell rocket:

HAPIfork contains an electronic key with a printed circuit that links the extremity of the fork and the handle of the fork. When you put the fork in the mouth, it closes the electronic loop. The device is able to count the number of fork servings during a meal because it only interacts with two parts of the body: your mouth and your hand.

That's right, folks, HAPIfork knows how long you take between bites, and if it's not long enough, this cutting-edge cutlery vibrates and flashes red lights to get you to slow down!

I know what you're thinking, bub: you have a wife to do that! But I'm here to tell you that HAPIfork is better than a wife because HAPIfork can't invite her mother to live with you for six months. That was a joke, ma'am.

Now, I ask you … how much would you be willing to pay for this amazing appliance, which will knock the weight off you faster than the Pittsburgh Pirates get knocked out of the pennant race every year? $300? $200?

Well, folks, find a place to sit down, because you are going to get weak in the knees when I tell you that I'm not asking $300, I'm not asking $200 … heck, folks, call me crazy, but I'm not asking even $100 for this terrific tined terror!

Preorder HAPIfork today, ladies and gents, and I'll charge you only $99. Plus, I'll throw in at absolutely no extra charge a software package that includes, in the words of the megabrained manufacturers of HAPIfork:

- An Online Dashboard to store and review your eating-related data and help you track your progress meal after meal
- A Mobile App so you can check your progress from the road as well as from home
- A Coaching Program to eat smarter and healthier: helpful, useful advice, practical tips and balanced meal plan
- A fun Online Social Game to motivate you to implement these new smart eating habits with your loved ones

Stick a HAPIfork in your eating problems, folks, because they're done!

But wait, there's more! Order today and I'll throw in, absolutely free (after a modest shipping and handling charge) your choice of these other fine products that the scientists in that tent over yonder are working on as we speak:

- SlottOmatic, the amazing perforated spoon that keeps you from eating too much soup!
- PointOmatic, the amazing electronic knife that tells you if you're holding it by the wrong end.

Act now! These products won't be around forever!

Keep yer mitts off the merchandise, kid!

Barbie Knows All, Sees All, Tells All

Author's note: This column first appeared in 2015.

I freely admit that I used to tie up the rubber Dale Evans figure from my Roy Rogers Chuck Wagon playset when I was a kid. In my imagination, Dale had been kidnapped by bad guys in an effort to force her husband, Roy, to relinquish control of the café he and Dale owned. Invariably, Roy and sidekick Pat Brady arrived in Pat's Jeep, Nellybelle, just in the nick of time to cut Dale loose before my mother asked why I had been using so much string lately.

I admit this early foray into bondage to establish my credentials. Yes, I played with dolls, so I'm qualified to comment knowledgeably about the latest nefarious threat to society: Hello Barbie.

Announced by toymaker Mattel in early March, Hello Barbie is a talking doll that somehow has flown under the radar of most national media — probably because the "Hello Donald" talking demagogue has captured their attention since its programmers had it announce its candidacy for president in mid-June.

But rather than making inflammatory statements to rile up its political base, Hello Barbie uses an implanted recording device to listen to what its owner says, then responds accordingly.

In order to have the doll record what is said to it (using a tiny microphone in her necklace), the user must press and hold Barbie's belt buckle. I don't know about that: In my experience, pressing and holding a woman's belt buckle will most likely produce a knee to the testicles.

On the phone with Dale in 1957 to say that we can marry now that Roy, at my left elbow, has gone to the last roundup.

But Hello Barbie is a bit more user friendly. She remembers users' preferences, such as a favorite color or what they want to be when they grow up, and she will respond in less than a second using up to 8,000 lines of pre-recorded dialog. No word on what response "Barbie, where did I hide my cigarettes?" might elicit.

Now, maybe parents of children who identify as female think it's a wonderful idea to have a doll that will engage in conversation while they themselves pursue more adult activities — texting or watching "Ridiculousness," for example. But they had better think twice: Hello Barbie is not only listening and recording what is said to her, she's also uploading that information to the Cloud via a wi-fi connection.

Mattel claims that storing the conversations allows Hello Barbie to tailor responses individually. Psychologists suggest that having a doll that responds in a realistic fashion might actually hinder a child's development of real friends. The more cynical among us see this as a chance for someone with evil designs — call him "Sleazy Uncle Ken" — to hack the information and use it against a child.

At the very least, Hello Barbie is a thinly veiled attempt at marketing research.

"Kids using 'Hello Barbie' aren't only talking to a doll, they are talking directly to a toy conglomerate whose only interest in them is financial," Susan Linn, former head of the organization Campaign for a Commercial-Free Childhood (CCFC), told CNN earlier this year. CFCC is attempting to block the release of Hello Barbie, which is set for November.

Protecting kids is great. But what's really needed is protection from marketers for gullible adults.

Anyone interested in a dozen blocks of mozzarella shaped like Pope Francis?

2013 A.Z.

When the zombies come to eat my brain, I suppose I'll be sorry if I don't buy Gerber's Apocalypse Survival Kit. It's a very cool thing. The description from the Gerber website:

"What if it happens? What if our worst fears are realized? If the Dead walk, the continuation of the human race will become a daily struggle. Are you prepared to protect and defend your family and friends? Your best chance lies in the Gerber Apocalypse Survival Kit. ... To beat the uprising we must work together. We must arm ourselves and organize."

The kit ($349) contains a camp axe, a military knife, two folding knives, a plain ol' machete, a "pro" machete and a machete called a parang—which I assume takes its name from the sound the blade makes when it lops off a zombie's head. Best of all, everything in the kit carries a lifetime warranty.

And you know that even after the zombies attack, Gerber—using all those kits in the warehouse to fend of the undead—will still be in business to replace your parang in case it chips on the skull of one of the walking dead. That's comforting. Yet, I hesitate.

The items in this kit are mostly for choppin', which means close combat. To keep my distance from zombies, I might want to spend my $349 on bullets. Not the Zombie Max ammo rolled out last year, but Jihawg Ammunition, being sold by South Fork Industries in Dalton Gardens, Idaho. Jihawg—coated with pork-infused paint—is being marketed as a double whammy against "Islamist terrorists."

"With Jihawg Ammo, you don't just kill an Islamist terrorist, you also send him to Hell," a South Fork press release states. "If it ever becomes necessary to defend yourself and those around you our ammo works on two levels." At just $24.75 per 50 rounds, I could at least hedge my bets just in case Islamist terrorist zombies show up. I mean, they were angry before they were dead.

My big question is, in order for Jihawg Ammo to work on two levels, doesn't an Islamist terrorist zombie need to know he's being shot with it? And won't my screaming, "I'm shooting you with a bullet laced with pork fat!" let said zombie lurch ever closer before I can get a round off? And if it does, will my replacement parang be back from Gerber yet? So, still, I hesitate.

And really—why would I want to survive the zombie apocalypse? I've seen the movies and TV shows. Constantly on the run. Afraid to sleep. Not knowing if I can trust other humans. OK—that doesn't sound so different from life as we know it now.

But think of the inconvenience!

You think it's hard to find toilet paper, bread and milk now before a predicted snowstorm? Just wait till 2013 A.Z. (After Zombie). We're talking, at best, day-old croissants and lukewarm lattes at Starbucks. Never having to send rental DVDs back to Netflix might even things out somewhat. But, honestly … one bar cellphone reception? Pu-leeze!

I think I don't want to survive the zombie apocalypse. Or an asteroid strike. Or nuclear war. So I'll ponder a bit more how to spend that $349.

Perhaps a DVD collection of Jerry Springer TV shows.

Then, if zombies do eat my brain, at least they'll get indigestion.

I read fake news today, oh boy ...

Let Me Entertain Yinz*

For several years, Dave wore the sparkling Mr. Entertainment cloak at his newspaper. But the man has a warped view of what is or is not entertaining. Reality television? Pedestrian. Musicians under the age of 56? Noisemakers. Professional athletes? Criminals on the hoof. A well-executed slip on a banana peel, though, convulses him. Shrewd word play from certain gifted writers causes spasms of ecstasy. And Donald Trump is always, always good for a hearty laugh. So here are Dave's cerebral ruminations on some celebrity phenomena. Just for the record: no Kardashians were harmed in the writing of these columns.

* Yinz is a Pittsburgh colloquialism used to indicate a group of two or more people.

Eenie, Meenie, Chili Beanie*

Author's note: This column first appeared in 1989.

You're standing around the office one day when someone says, "How'd you like to be a celebrity judge at the Super Bowl of Chile?"

You accept. You're flattered to be called a celebrity, you enjoy soccer and, hey, you've always wanted to see South America. You hope to get Pele's autograph.

When they tell you to report to Washington Mall** at 3:15 p.m. February 3, you figure it's to catch the shuttle to Greater Pittsburgh Airport.

You arrive early, overnight bag in hand, "SOCCER TO ME BABY" T-shirt on torso. You're psyched.

But then the someone who recruited you says you're judging the Super Bowl of *Chili,* not Chile, that soccer is not even remotely involved, that the only South you'll see is South Strabane Township and that you're going to taste 50-odd bowls of semi-viscous concoctions the ingredients of which their cooks would not reveal, even under torture. Not because the ingredients are secret, but because the cooks can't remember what they are.

You run. You're caught.

"Well," you think as they introduce you, "it can't be as bad as airline food."

Then you notice the Haz-Mat team is hosing down the floor beneath the table reserved for "hottest chilies." There's a ragged hole, its rim smoking, in the tablecloth. And the table. The event organizer tells you that's your category. You start to cry.

"Cheer up," another celebrity judge tells you. "Blue Cross covered my entire hospital stay last year."

You grin bravely, then bribe a passing kid to go and buy some antacid. He takes your $20. He does not return.

The moment of judgment arrives. "The hotter the better, eh, buddy?" a third judge asks, elbowing you. You notice he's wearing an asbestos apron.

"You bet!" you reply. But you're ashamed to admit your wife's chili, made from a family recipe handed down through generations, consists of ground beef, kidney beans and tomato soup. Ice is hotter.

But you're trapped. You taste from bowl one. Your eyes water. Your eyebrows begin to sweat after bowl two. Bowl three produces some really neat blisters on your tongue. By bowl four, you realize you're going to have to swallow before you can fit spoonful five into your mouth.

You swallow. You immediately realize how the good people of Pompeii felt after Mt. Vesuvius erupted.

After bowl 22, the Pittsburgh Steeler seated next to you cries out, "Send in the second team!"

Bowl 23 contains an oil slick roughly twice the size of the one Saddam Hussein dumped into the Persian Gulf. Out of the corner of your eye, you notice the Haz-Mat team readying absorbent booms.

You glance to your left, where three judges are sampling chili with beans.

"Lucky them," you think. Then you notice two have taken on the look of the Hindenberg just before its arrival at Lakehurst, New Jersey. Mall security guards are attempting to tether them to steel posts driven into the floor.

After bowl 35, you look to your right, toward the judges tasting Texas-style chili.

"Yum," you think. Lots of big, chunky gobs of meat jockeying for position in each bowl.

"This is great!" one of those judges says. "What kind of meat is this?" Before anyone can answer, a spectator screams, "My Chihuahua is missing!" One of the cooks awaiting the judges' decision begins to roll his eyes toward the ceiling and whistle. You swear there's a rhinestone collar protruding from the back pocket of his jeans.

Hottest chili seems not so bad now. Twelve spoonsful later, you're buzzing, high on cayenne pepper.

"Wild tattoo," a fellow judge says, pointing to your left bicep.

"Huh?" you say, bleary eyed. You inspect the skin. Chili has splattered from your spoon, turning what previously had been a smallpox-vaccination scar into a replica of da Vinci's "Last Supper."

Soon the judging is over. Justice is served: the City of Washington Fire Department wins first prize in the "hottest" category. Grateful, they douse your flaming beard before claiming their plaque.

The paramedics are gentle. As the ambulance passes a restaurant, you catch a glimpse of the kid you sent to buy antacid.

He's eating prime rib.

* This title is drawn from "The Adventures of Rocky and Bullwinkle," another of my favorite shows as a kid and a wonderful source of puns.

** That's Washington, Pa., a small city south of Pittsburgh and home to the Pony League World Series.

The Buzz About Buzz

Author's note: This column was the first to appear when I began writing again in 2010.

Imagine my surprise when, last Tuesday, I actually knew what happened the night before on "Dancing with the Stars" (DWTS).

Bear in mind that I don't watch "reality shows." If watching Paul McCartney's gold-digging, one-and-a-half-legged ex-wife, Heather Mills, hobble around the dance floor for six weeks qualifies as reality, I'll pass. (C'mon—you watched because you hoped her prosthetic gam would fall off, not because your soul drips terpsichore.*)

But on April 6, former astronaut Buzz Aldrin was booted from DWTS after appearing for only two weeks. The next morning, news of Aldrin's premature ejection featured prominently in newscasts. I viewed this as a good thing because it meant that no Pittsburgh Steelers had yet been arrested that day. And that we'd probably won the War on Terror.

But then I started to feel sorry for poor ol' Buzz. Here's a guy who gets less respect than Rodney Dangerfield. It began when Neil Armstrong grabbed the title "First Man on the Moon" not so much because he had seniority over Aldrin, but because the hatch of the Eagle moon lander opened inward, trapping Buzz, its pilot, behind the door. And behind the eight ball as "Second Man on the Moon."

This title isn't quite as bad as being the instantly forgettable Damon Berryhill. Berryhill was on base behind Sid Bream when Bream scored the winning run for the Atlanta Braves in the seventh game of the 1992 NLCS against the Pittsburgh Pirates. Being Second Man on the Moon rightly commands more notoriety. But it doesn't stop people from viewing Buzz as No. 2 in all things. And, thus, slightly less worthy.

"Forty years later, Buzz Aldrin is still the second man out," was the lead of a story by *Space.com* writer Robert Z. Pearlman the morning after the DWTS episode.

Aldrin took it on the chin again after endorsing President Obama's plan to land men on Mars rather than send them back to the moon, a plan favored by—who else?—Neil Armstrong. I have to wonder, why is Armstrong so hot to send men back to the moon? Did he forget his wallet?

But media mavens made Aldrin's stamp of approval a lesser thing than Armstrong's. No respect, I tell ya ...

So I'm going to explain why Buzz—the Avis Rent-A-Car of space—deserves our respect:

1.   He didn't attempt to moonwalk on DWTS.
2.   He isn't shilling for Priceline like fake astronaut William Shatner.
3.   Buzz Lightyear ("Toy Story") was named after Aldrin. Neil Lightyear? I think not.
4.   He walked on the moon. Did you?

Here's to you, Buzz. And to the day when no one really cares who was tossed from DWTS.

That will truly be one giant leap for mankind.

* *Terpsichore was the Greek Muse of dance.*

Writing Naked

I'm not wearing pants.

This is not one of former U.S. Rep. Anthony Weiner's favorite texting lines. It is merely a statement of fact. Working from home has its perks. When your office is a back bedroom, you needn't shower, shave or brush your teeth. Nor do you need to wear pants. Ask my neighbors.

OK, I've been both above-board and below-waist with you. Whether we take our relationship to the next level is up to you. I'm thinking of making this a naked column. The premise is simple: I write in the nude, you read in the nude.

I got this idea from reality TV. In case you haven't noticed, there's a whole slew of cable shows in which the participants are nude: The Discovery Channel's "Naked and Afraid"; VH-1's "Dating Naked"; TLC's "Buying Naked."

Of course full-frontal nudity is blurred on these shows because everyone knows that seeing below-the-equator frontal naughty bits makes the heads of Americans explode. Exactly why it doesn't produce the same response in people from other countries has something to do with either their drinking water or socialized medicine. Maybe that's why Republicans hate Obamacare. Naked butts, naturally, are OK on American TV because they only make us laugh. Where do you think the phrase "butt of a joke" came from?

"Naked and Afraid," the first program of its type in America, dumps one naked male and one naked female in an extreme environment for 21 days. A clothed, provisioned camera crew accompanies the couple but cannot interfere except in case of medical emergency. Each participant is permitted to choose one survival tool—a machete, perhaps, or flint with which to make a fire. Me, I'd choose an AK-47 with a full clip—to kill animals for food. But if that didn't work, I'd shoot out the cameras, steal the crew's food and claim I came through on wits alone.

As you might expect, the survivalists complain a lot and go against type. A military vet succumbs to sunburn and is rescued by his hard-as-nails female companion, who inexplicably is filled with remorse over having to kill an eel for food. Curiously, she shows no remorse over having to strip off on TV to feel self-worth.

The premise of "Dating Naked" is clear from its title—a man and a woman go on a date and, at least initially, neither wears clothes. One male participant becomes jealous when his date pays more attention to another naked guy; one woman becomes angry because her date fails to protect her from being whacked in the eye by a tree branch while they partake of naked zip-lining. It's the stuff of high school dating except that, for men, it's really hard to decide where to pin the corsage on prom night.

Needless to say, the ratings for all the "naked" shows are through the roof. I figure I'd best start "Writing Naked" before it shows up on MTV.

So, readers, what d'ya say? I'll start writing naked if you'll start reading naked. Who knows where this could lead? Naked book clubs? Naked poetry readings? Naked Amazon reviews? We'll begin in two weeks. It will be liberating for all of us.

It will also be BYOC: Bring Your Own Chair.

One caveat: avoid vinyl.

All in the Family

Dave does not exactly wear his heart on his sleeve. Occasionally, you can catch sight of it just above the suede elbow patch on his corduroy jacket. That's where these columns come from—uncommon from-the-heart musings about kith and kin.

'M' Is for the Memories She Gave Me

Author's note: This column first appeared in 1991.

Your father forgets when he was young," she said, stroking the blubbering boy's hair.

He heard her words, but wept on. Slumped on her lap, his face pressed hard against her bosom, the boy stained his mother's flowered dress with lukewarm tears. She set the chair rocking and began to sing, barely audibly:

Marizy doats, and dozy doats.
And little lambsie divey.
A kiddle ee divey too,
Wooden shoe?*

The words made no sense to the boy. He liked them. When he awoke the next morning, he had forgotten his tears. But 37 years later, as Mother's Day approached, a 42-year-old-man remembered. And smiled.

*   *   *

Dear Mom,

Sorry I never write, but I write for a living and don't feel much like it when I get home. Does a steelworker go back to the mill to relax on his day off?

Sorry I haven't called for so long, but I'm on the phone a lot at work. That line about the steelworker? Same goes for a telephone operator.

Sorry we haven't visited for so long, too. But there's only so much time in the weekend.

Sorry, Mom, Sorry I haven't been much of a son lately. But I haven't forgotten you. I haven't forgotten when I was young.

* * *

In a green-lidded box in the bottom drawer of his son's dresser

are pictures—not-very-good pictures taken by a not-very-good photographer wielding a not-very-good camera. Faded color pictures, clasped in a flimsy yellow cardboard binder with the word "Kodak" etched in red on its cover. Freeze-frames of his youth.

Here are his model airplanes, arrayed on the purple bedspread/runway of the double bed that clogged his sister's room. Here is his dog, a black cocker spaniel he named Spooky. Why, here he is, at 8, wearing summer pajamas and a multicolored beanie bedecked with the whistles, whirligigs and plastic miniature race cars that all young boys hold precious.

And here, in the very last photo, is his mother, wearing a shin-length blue nightgown, standing in the tiled upstairs hallway of the little white house on 13th Street. Spooky obscures her bare feet. On her head the boy's beanie rests lopsidedly; from her mouth her tongue sticks sassily. It is his favorite picture of his mother. When he closes his eyes and thinks of Esther, this is the first image he sees.

Hello?
Hi! It's me. I haven't forgotten you.
Is this David or Harold?
Dave.
You sound so much alike.
How are you feeling?
I think I had a stroke.
WHAT?
I'm all right now.
What do you mean, a stroke?
I had a pain in my chest.
How long ago?
Two days, I think. Yes. Thursday.
Did you call the doctor?
What did you say?
Did you call the doctor?
I can't hear you.
Do you have your hearing aids in?
I don't have my hearing aids in.
I thought so.
(PAUSE) I can't hear you.
WE'RE … COMING … DOWN.
You don't have to.
YES, I DO.
I'll be here.

*   *   *

When he was 18 and she 55, she helped him run away from home.**

He had come in after midnight after being out with friend on a Sunday night—something his father strictly forbade. Clad in boxer shorts and a sleeveless undershirt, the old man confronted him and said, "If you don't like it here, you can leave."

So he had gone upstairs and begun to pack a suitcase. Hearing this, his father had climbed the stairs and renewed the argument.

Then his mother had appeared in the tiled hallway behind his father.

"Barney, stop."

"Go ahead and stick up for him," his father had said before stomping down the stairs.

"What are you doing with that?" his mother had asked, pointing to the suitcase.

"Leaving."

"Don't go, David. Do it for me."

He had weakened momentarily, but could not back down.

"Where will you go?" his mother had asked.

"I don't know."

"Wait. I'll drive you."

Stunned, he had followed her to the family car.

"Your father forgets when he was young," she said.

*   *   *

Yes, Mom. But you haven't.
And I haven't forgotten you.
I haven't forgotten when I was young.

* *Editor's note: This novelty song from the 1940s was written by Milton Drake, Al Hoffman and Jerry Livingston. The sheet music features the nonsense syllables for the chorus, but the bridge translates them as:*
> *Mares eat oats, and does eat oats,*
> *And little lambs eat ivy*
> *A kid'll eat ivy, too,*
> *Wouldn't you?*

** *For a full recounting of this incident, see "Childhood's End," in the* Essays *section of this book.*

Like Mother, Like Son

Author's note: This column first appeared in 1993. It is one of three for which I won the Keystone Press Award in 1994.

For every man who sees his father's face staring back at him from the medicine-chest mirror each morning, another sees his mother's. Mama's boys, they're called. Count me among them.

Because of Mom, I am what I am. But, like many of my generation, I have not yet adopted my final form. Whatever shape I eventually settle on, though, Mom will have had a hand in molding it. And like the best sculptors, she exerted only minute pressure.

Mom took each of life's setbacks with the measured stride of a Marine fresh from boot camp. Nothing stopped her; nothing surprised her. In these ways, I am exactly like her.

"It's always somethin'," Mom would say when the latest monkey wrench turned up in the works, perhaps with a sigh, but never with bitterness. Then, having said it, she'd remove the wrench, grease the gears and set the machine in motion again.

Arthritis hit Mom hard when she was in her late 60s, and it was by far the largest monkey wrench she had encountered. She handled it like a master mechanic. Two years ago, though, when she turned 79, the wrench became inextricably wedged in the cogs. Mom left it there. Eventually, she knew, the gears grind to a halt for all of us.

These things Mom taught me:

- Cast not the first stone.
- Forget not when you were young.
- Fail not to talk often with your mother; if you do, you will wish you had after she is gone.

And one more thing.

When I was a child and impatiently waiting for some major even—the arrival of summer vacation or, perhaps, my birthday—I'd often say, "I wish it would hurry up and get here!"

"Don't wish your life away!" Mom would chide. "When you get older, the days are shorter."

I didn't believe her. Of course, she was right.

I'm 44 now. January blends easily into December; the strains of Christmas carols seem to be heard once more almost before the echoes of "Auld Land Syne" have faded. The days *are* shorter; time *does* move more quickly. So quickly, in fact, that in the last two years Mom seemed to have aged a decade. Pictures show it clearly now. Somehow, I never noticed.

I visited Mom at the hospital on Easter. She'd been in the place, on and off, for seven of the last 14 months. Not much was new. But we talked, in the halting manner that is the hallmark of our family, for about an hour. She looked well; she sounded terrible.

"How long have you had this cough?" I asked.

"Oh, about two weeks," she said. "The daughter of the woman

who was in here with me before had a cold and coughed all the time when she came to visit. It's always somethin'."

Mom and I never talked after that; the ventilating tube they'd put down her throat made conversation impossible. But I talked, and she nodded or shook her head, as the question demanded.

Every so often, she would look up at the machines surrounding her—at the tubes and wires looping from them to her arms and fingers and chest and nose and mouth—then roll her eyes and shake her head.

"It's always somethin'," I knew she was thinking. This time, it was pneumonia.

Mom died Monday.

Since then, the days have seemed not nearly so short.

Home Again, Home Again

Author's note: This column first appeared in 1993.

Like most kids who grow up and move out of their parents' home, I left behind decades' worth of prized possessions that I just couldn't bear to part with until it became obvious I had no room for them in my new house.

As the years passed, I had fully intended to retrieve them. But there is no more convenient form of long-term storage than that for which you do not pay. So they languished there, in closets and attics and dresser drawers and, probably, under my old twin bed. I would retrieve them, I told myself, on that famous date that never has and never will appear on any calendar: Someday.

Someday came May 3, when my 81-year-old mother died, forcing me to come to grips nor only with my own mortality but with something even more dreadful: sorting through my junk. My sister had handled the estate and most of the busy work, separating those items which might be of sentimental value to me and my

47

brothers, then donating the rest to charities. After a few months, I made what I knew would be my final trip "home."

I figured it would take me most of the day, what with my being unable to part with items that had helped me through childhood and adolescence. And there would be many. I made sure to take the big sedan because I knew I'd need the trunk room.

All my record albums are there, I thought on the hour-long drive. *All my books, my DayGlo posters. Maybe my first pair of Beatle boots is still there … and my first-baseman's mitt. My fringed buckskin jacket!*

All that valuable stuff! Yeah, this was going to take all day.

Three hours later, I walked back into my own home, carrying everything of value I'd found at the old homestead: a pair of wooden salad tongs, a wire cake rack and a 9 x 13 metal baking pan.

Oh, most of that other stuff had been there, all right. The Monkees' first LP; albums by bands I once must have loved but now did not recognize; enough books to outfit a small library. A football helmet; a baseball glove; train sets. My college band uniform—someone's tuition probably increased to cover that oversight. Treasures become trash.

"Burn, toss or otherwise dispose of this junk as you see fit," I wrote in a note to my sister. "It means nothing to me and I can't imagine why it ever did."

True, each item when held in my hand doubtless would have spurred some memory, painful, joyous or bittersweet. But I already had those. There was the corner where our chrome Christmas tree stood each yuletide from 1960 until 1970, when I left home for the first time. I'd come back four years later, tail between legs, bringing with me only what could fit in a Volkswagen Beetle. There was the doorway where Dad had fallen dead … after I shot him with my cap pistol. There was the stairway where Mom sat huddled during thunderstorms because she was terrified of lightning. I knew this place.

I found a lesson, too. Accumulate all the material things you want. But when Someday comes, take the memories.

For one thing, they'll all fit in a Volkswagen.

Suddenly, Last Winter

Author's note: This column first appeared in 2011.

A house," comedian George Carlin riffed, "is just a pile of stuff with a cover on it." Exactly how accurate that observation is became clear to me around 3 p.m. Sunday. That's when I stood in a driveway in Michigan, staring at all that was left of my brother Harry's worldly goods.

Harry, age 22

My senior by 14 years, Harry died in February. Although "unexpectedly" is the way I characterized his death in the obituary I wrote for him, I don't think it's the correct term. Harry would have preferred "suddenly," a romantic, Tennessee Williams-like word that perfectly describes how it happened. Death came not as the feeble, lingering flicker of a candle, but as the rapid evanescence of photons after the flick of a switch. I think that's how he wanted it.

I am now in charge of my brother's estate as what Michigan calls his "Personal Representative." He would like this designation, and so do I. An executor executes. But a PR represents a person. I hope I represent him accurately.

Harry was what people once called a "Renaissance Man." He worked through high school as an auto body man, hammering out what careless drivers had hammered in. He played trombone and upright bass and by 18 had mastered music theory, mostly by reading books and working it out on his own. Drafted in the late 1950s, he spent two years in Army bands in France and Germany, the premiere hot jazz trombonist in bands that hot jazz trombonists fought to join.

My brother relaxed by writing big band arrangements that he kept in his head, never once having to touch a piano to check his work. A jazz musician is what he wanted to be and what he should have been. But rock music effectively ended that dream. So he became a psychologist. And, just as with music, Harry mastered the art.

Although he had a PhD and could have taught in a university, Harry spent his entire career working with learning-disabled kids in Michigan public schools. Co-workers say he was damned good at it, too. He won awards for excellence as editor of a statewide publication for school psychologists. In summers he dragged a "fifth wheel" trailer behind a 1979 Ford pickup that he kept immaculate. He helped to design the house he had built 22 years ago, then finished much of the interior himself. Meticulous and analytical, he packed four-drawer file cabinets with information about every facet of almost any subject you can think of.

Among his favorite subjects: handyman tips; camping; computing; diet; exercise; railroads; airplanes; cars; psychology; history; politics; making your own environmentally friendly cleaning products; installing a gas fireplace; DIY Internet wiring.

By the time we inventoried his possessions, we had filled 47 18-gallon Rubbermaid storage bins with clippings, books, magazines, sheet music, LPs, DVDs, CDs and VHS tapes.

"Man," the auctioneer who set up the estate sale said as we walked through Harry's house, "your brother was good at everything!"

That he was. But he was best at being a brother.

We shared a bedroom until I was 9 years old. He didn't tell my parents when I "borrowed" the dirty pictures he had brought back from France. He taught me to pick up after myself, to iron my own clothes, to do my own laundry. He bought my first trombone and taught me to play it. He stayed up late with me to laugh at "The Tonight Show" with Steve Allen. He took me to drive-in movies and turned off the speaker; then we made up our own dialog.

When I was 16 and decided to be a rock star, he defended my choice to our dad. When I was out of work, he sent money; he never asked to be paid back. He listened to me when I needed to talk. He told me the truth. He stayed in touch.

The Michiganders who came to the estate auction on Saturday carried away almost everything my brother had accumulated, leaving me standing in the driveway Sunday with roughly 12 garbage bags, several cardboard boxes and one plastic bucket harboring a well-used sump pump. Harry's stuff.

But not Harry.

He rode home with me.

Scenes From a Marriage

Author's note: This column elicited irate calls and letters from readers. I like to believe it was because when they got to the end, they felt cheated because they were expecting something lascivious.

H ow long has it been since we ... you know!" his wife asked.
"If you have to ask, it has been too long," he replied.
"I know, I know," she said.
They both laughed.
But it had been too long.
In fact, all he could recall was that the last time he had done it, it was with her.
Time was they had done it regularly—even before they were married, if the truth be known. Even in the afternoon.
They continued apace during their first three years of marriage. They had done it almost every weekend then.
They had enjoyed it so much on one occasion that they had held hands and cried in the dark after it was over.

Then he had changed jobs.

He had begun working evenings and weekends. She, working daylight, was often asleep when he arrived home from work.

They began to do it less frequently.

*   *   *

Often during this period they would go to parties or picnics, listen to their friends talk about doing it, and recall how much they had enjoyed the experience—the flicker of lights turned low; the whisper of soft music.

Sometimes, their memories stirred by what they had heard, they would excuse themselves early from the party or picnic, drive away and do it. If the hour was late, they might wait until the next day. But do it they would. Always.

And always they could remember when the last time had been.

Then, after nearly eight years of marriage, things had changed again. Drastically.

She had become pregnant; he had begun working night turn. They seldom saw each other.

And if they did, almost by accident, manage to spend a weekend evening together, they often were too tired to do it.

Before long, reading about it was all they did.

After the baby was born—after a nine-month stretch when, if memory served, they had done it but once—they had made special arrangements to do it.

They had had to: She would be returning to work. They knew the chance would not soon come again—she, working daylight, would definitely be asleep when he arrived home from work.

So they did it—left their infant son with her sister for a few hours, drove off and did it. They both still remembered that time.

But the baby grew and doing it became even more difficult. They thought about scheduling a time for it, but both wanted it to be spontaneous. Besides, they thought, what if it's bad? Then what do we do? So they postponed it.

Soon neither could recall the last time they had done it.

*   *   *

Not that they had forgotten how to do it. They often sat watching a rented movie in the family room and talked about doing it again. But they never quite got around to actually doing it.

Finally, she had called him at work.

"How long has it been since we … you know?" she asked.

"If you have to ask, it has been too long," he replied.

"I know it was during the day … and that we liked it," he continued, digging deep into his memory. "But geez … I don't know when it was."

He laughed. "Maybe we should start writing it down on the calendar."

"Ha!" she had said sarcastically. So he had decided not to mention it for a while.

Besides, he knew, vacation was coming. They would be together every day and night for a week. No more excuses. They would do it. They would leave their son with her sister again if they had to.

And if that proved impossible, they would let the boy watch.

After all, he was now almost 2½—a babe-in-arms no more. Anyway, he'd never remember what he saw. And even if he did, he'd never understand it.

Yes. They'd do it while they were on vacation.

They'd go out to a movie.

Even if they both had headaches.

Not From My Side of the Family

Author's note: This column first appeared in 1991. My son Steve turned 28 in 2017.

"I told you wait a minute!" he heard the voice say.

He had seen his father use the stance a thousand times. A lecture was coming.

But the lecturer was his 2½-year-old son.

"No change diaper! I told you wait a minute!"

"I'm the father! I say when we change diapers," he said.

"Daddy, I told you no."

"I say yes."

"I say no."

He huffed out some air and took a step toward his son.

The boy whirled, galloped into the living room and threw himself headlong onto the couch, giggling.

"No get me!" his son screamed.

Placing a hand under each of the boy's armpits, he lifted his son from the couch. The boy snapped both arms toward the ceiling and slithered free.

He knew the ritual well by now. He would stalk the boy; the boy would elude him. Finally, he would threaten to leave without his son and the diaper would be changed. The scene went as scripted.

"OK, buddy," he said after the ritual. "Let's go to Winnie's."

"Daddy stay with Stevie," the boy pouted.

"I can't," he replied. "We have to go."

"I can't," his son said.

He sighed. Being a father was hard work.

*   *   *

Actually, not everything about being a father was hard work. He still could beat his son in a footrace, if only because his legs were longer. He still could lift his son using only one arm, still could secure two kicking legs by placing one hand around both the boy's ankles. Those things were easy.

What was hard was trying to outthink the kid.

"Where does he pick up this stuff?" he had asked his wife after the boy started using a four-letter word.

"Punk!" the boy had said.

"Steve, don't call people that," he had told the boy. "It's not nice!"

The boy had smiled. "Punk!"

"Stephen!"

"Bunk ... dunk... hunk..."

"Stop that!"

"... lunk ... munk ... sunk ..."

"Please?"

"... wunk ..."

"STEVE!"

"I'm sorry, Daddy."

"That's better." The boy had run from the room.

"Where does he pick up this stuff?" he had asked his wife.

"Not from me."

Maybe from the babysitter's boy, he had thought.

"Go get him ready for bed," his wife had suggested.

"OK," he had said.

"C'mere, punk," his wife had heard him say from the next room.

*   *   *

He remembered standing in the basement of his boyhood home, watching his father work on the old black Rambler.

"Go get me the hammer," his father had said.

He had gone to the red-painted workbench, pulled off a square-headed hammer and walked back to where his father's feet protruded from under the car.

"Here," he had said, holding out the hammer.

His father had not answered.

"Here," he had said again.

His father had grunted.

"Here, Dad, here," he had said, hopping from one foot to the other.

His father had squirmed out from under the station wagon.

"For God's sake, put it down! Don't stand there and say, 'Here!' like an idjit! Put it down! Put it down!"

He had dropped the hammer on his father's foot.

*   *   *

"Here, Dad, here!" the boy said.

He did not answer.

"Daddy, here!" the boy said, holding out a screwdriver.

59

He grunted.

"Daddy, h-e-e-r-r-e-e!"

"Stephen, put it down! Put it down! Don't just stand there whining! Put it down!"

The boy threw the screwdriver.

"Do not throw things! Do you understand me? It's not nice to throw things! You'll hurt somebody!"

The boy began to cry and ran to his mother.

"Honey, you know it's not nice to throw things!" she said. "Tell Daddy you're sorry"

"I'm sorry, Daddy."

He hugged his son. Later, after the boy had fallen asleep in his lap, he carried him to bed, kissed him and walked back downstairs.

"Where does he pick up this stuff?" he asked his wife while rolling his socks into a ball.

"Not from me," she answered.

The socks hit her square in the forehead.

WE WILL, WE WILL
ROCK THEE...

A Dedicated Follower of Fashion*

Molter is not noted for his fashion sense. At a recent classic rock concert, Dave played bass, and his sartorial splendor earned him the squealing adoration of a group of Mennonite women — a group that included a mom and her 9 or 12 or 17 daughters. They all wore traditional dresses and bonnets, which made it hard to take an accurate head count. I believe that night Dave wore his purple boots with the Cuban heels. Anyway, after the concert, the gals waited for Dave to descend from the stage and into their dreams. Apparently, there was no prohibition against cameras in their particular sect, and Dave, the brilliantly plumed male peacock in the midst of the drab peahens, happily posed with his Luddite fans for photos.

Think about the sort of manly attire that might set buggy riders' hearts a-throbbin, and you'll be able to put these columns into context.

*The Kinks, 1965

Dead Man Walking

As he sat down to write his weekly column, he was wearing a dead man's shoes.

"Hey, what size shoes do you wear?" his sister-in-law's husband's father had asked several weeks earlier.

"Nine-and-a-half," he had answered.

"Well, I got a pair of Florsheims right here in this box that should fit you. Try them on."

"Great," he had said.

The shoes were the type that, as a teenager, he had sworn never to wear—black, clunky things with skinny laces, almost wingtips. The kind of shoes his teachers had worn, not at all like the cool, Cuban-heeled Beatle boots that quite literally carried him through high school.

But these shoes had one overwhelmingly attractive element – no price tag. So on his feet they had gone.

"They fit," he had said.

"They're yours," his sister-in-law's husband's father had replied. "The guy who owned them's dead."

The shoes suddenly felt strange.

"What did he die from?" he had asked.

"He had a heart attack while bending over to tie his shoes," his sister-in-law's husband had said, jokingly.

"Ha, ha, ha," he had laughed. Then he slipped the shoes off and back into their box, wrapped a rubber band around its lid and carried them home.

One day later, he had worn them to work.

"Look," he had told one of his female co-workers. "I'm wearing ... (dramatic pause) ... dead man's shoes." Then he had done a Fred Astaire shuffle.

"Oh? How nice! What killed him?" she asked.

"He had a heart attack while bending over to tie them," he had said, trying out the purloined joke.

"I thought maybe he died of a contagious foot disease," she had said, without so much as a smirk.

"Ha, ha, ha," he had laughed, enjoying the joke. But later that night, his right foot had begun to itch.

That weekend, while lounging on the loveseat, doing his TV-remote-control-digit aerobics, he had stumbled across a "Twilight Zone" rerun. "Dead Man's Shoes," the episode was called.

In it, a man stole a pair of spiffy kicks from a corpse—without knowing the dead man had been a gangster. The drifter laced on the shoes and, suddenly, had a whole different walk of life.

In short, the shoes possessed the drifter. He took up with the dead gangster's moll, began to strongarm the enemies of the shoes' former owner. Finally, he confronted the man who had murdered the gangster. Who promptly killed the drifter.

The show closed with the body of the drifter—still wearing the shoes—being dumped in an alley, where a wino noticed the corpse's spiffy kicks. And stole them and laced them on.

"Ha, ha, ha," he had laughed as the credits rolled. But later that night, as he drifted off to sleep, he thought he heard the shoes shuffling around the bedroom. In the morning, their tongues stuck out at him.

That day he received a phone call from an unknown woman.

"Is Johnny there?"

"Sorry, wrong number," he had answered. But he thought he heard machine-gun fire in the background. And out of the corner of his eye as he was hanging up, he thought he saw the shoes padding out of the kitchen doorway.

Time passed. He forgot about the dead man's shoes. But as he sat down to write his weekly column, he realized they were on his feet. He tried to write the heartwarming column he had planned—about his walk through downtown Washington on the first day of spring—but it refused to be written.

It was then he realized that he had sold his soles to the devil.

Getting a Jeg Up on Fashion

C lothes make the man," is a statement variously attributed to, among others, Homer (not Simpson), William Shakespeare and Moses (Leibowitz, my tailor).

In its original form, the statement conveys the idea that how a man dresses plays a large role in how people perceive him. But as rewritten for the 21st century by some school administrators, the phrase now apparently should be, "Clothes make the man horny."

The latest example of this train of thought comes from North Dakota, where the assistant principal at the aptly named Devil's Lake High School has banned female students from wearing leggings, super-tight skinny jeans called "jeggings" and yoga pants. The rule was put into place, the principal said, because such attire is too distracting to not only male students, but also to male teachers.

Make no mistake about it: I'm in favor of school dress codes, even school dress codes gone wrong. Given no guidelines, some kids would no doubt show up wearing Saran Wrap with bits of Reynolds Wrap placed strategically.

My experience with a dress code that still seems silly involves my junior high school's ban on girls wearing nylons with tennis shoes, as if dress shoes somehow canceled out the irresistible, lust-causing sight of a 15-year-old girl's ankle. The same administrators apparently thought that a glimpse of a cheerleader's color-coordinated panties under her mid-thigh-length pleated skirt as it rose to her waist during a spin inspired in boys only the irresistible desire to score more points on the gridiron or basketball court. Short-sighted, indeed.

But no matter how you look at it, the action at Devil's Lake (and in many other school districts across America) fails in one key way: it places responsibility — and blame — on females only.

To illustrate the point behind the legwear ban, the Devil's Lake administrator screened two clips from the film "Pretty Woman," in which Julia Roberts, portraying a prostitute, wears tight-fitting legwear. It's a theorem for the modern age:

1. Prostitutes wear tight-fitting legwear.
2. Your daughter wears tight-fitting legwear.
3. Your daughter is a prostitute.

Pity the poor male *homo sapiens*: discoverer of fire and conqueror of land, sea and air, still he cannot control himself when confronted with the sight of a female of the species wearing tight or revealing clothing.

Here's another old saying: What a load of crap!

Thinking such as this has its origins in the belief that Adam was doing just fine until Eve force-fed him The Apple. It's the same kind of flawed reasoning that says a woman who is raped while wearing a short skirt "asked for it," or that a woman abused by her male partner must have done something to provoke him.

Worse, it's the kind of skewed reasoning that allows men to avoid taking responsibility for their own actions by neatly shifting the blame to someone society is more comfortable condemning.

"She made me do it." Falls trippingly on the tongue, does it not?

Adam thought so.

Manning Up in Century 21

My inner English major grimaced last week when I read about the death of the Metrosexual. Not having paid much attention to pop culture for the past 20 years, I hadn't heard the term before. I figured it was one of those made-up words like "abdicake," which means "To give up the last piece of cake to someone else."

So I took a quick look at the root of the word and decided that "Metrosexual" must mean someone interested in sex in the subway. I was wrong.

A Metrosexual, urban dictionaries tell us, is a man who cares about his appearance and takes an interest in fashion, art and culture. He is more likely to go to a hair salon than to drift into a one-chair barbershop and grunt, "All over with a No. 1 clipper." He has more than two pairs of shoes. He is conversant in many subjects, from baseball (Batter up!) to the best way to avoid having your soufflé fall (Batter down!).

In short, a Metrosexual is not overtly "manly"—at least not in the classic 1950s "strong, silent type" sense. So, many American males between the ages of 25 and 40 now have declared him dead.

They're calling it the "Menaissance" and passing out cigars to celebrate the birth of the "Retrosexual." Oh, my!

I grew up in the Fifties, but I've never been particularly good at being male. I had all the requisite male accoutrements: toy guns, trucks, trains, baseball gear. I was dipped early and often in testosterone. It dripped right off.

By the time I was 16 in 1965, manhood had been in a constant state of flux for three years. Was James Bond a man? Of course—he carried a gun, drove a fast car and treated women as sex objects. But Bond also may have been Metrosexual Prime: he dressed well; he could judge the temperature of a magnum of Chateau Lafite-Rothschild just by looking at it. Were the Beatles men? Of course, but they broke all the male grooming and fashion rules and had a flair for the arts. It was a confusing time in which to come of age.

Thus, by the early 1970s, wearing bell-bottoms and a fringed buckskin jacket and with my hair hanging past my shoulders, I was often mistaken for a girl. This was the time when men and women dressed virtually identically—the era of "Best Ask: Can't Tell."

Yet despite all this, I knew I was a man. Apparently those behind the Menaissance movement aren't so lucky. A couple of Retrosexual bloggers claim that women's lib started all the trouble.

Strong, capable women in positions of power, they say, make unclear what qualities comprise manliness in 2010. So they're running headlong for the perceived sanctuary of an era they are familiar with only through watching "Mad Men." Thank God they haven't been watching "Spartacus."

Brothers, manhood is something you shape to fit yourself, not vice versa. Manhood cannot be bought. It cannot be packaged. And it certainly can't be bottled.

Despite what those Old Spice "Smell like a man, man" commercials tell you, it's still body wash. You're big on being manly? Use Comet and Wet-or-Dry sandpaper in the shower.

Then you'll be a man with true grit.

Gender Gap Sap

When it comes to gender sensitivity, Dave is an equal-opportunity offender. He admits that throughout his life, most of his deep, long-lasting friendships have been with women, but there are some guys that have hung in there with him, too. He's a closet feminist who doesn't like to see anyone pushed around because of their interpretation of what it means to be masculine or feminine or something else. But he likes to point out the humor and the inconsistency because that's just what he does.

Ho Ho Homophobic

Author's note: This column first appeared in 2013.

Pity poor Hallmark. Seeking to avoid being perceived as a company marketing a Christmas ornament that might be offensive to some, the greeting cards giant instead has offended almost everyone.

In late October, Hallmark rolled out a Christmas ornament patterned after the gaudy multicolored holiday sweaters that revelers unabashedly wear in the month of December. Great idea! Except that the company made one slight change in the lyrics of a line from the carol "Deck the Halls" that appear on the ornament. Rather than "Don we now our gay apparel," the ornament text reads, "Don we now our *fun* apparel."

Perhaps the designers thought the change would go unnoticed. But it took only a few days for Christmas traditionalists and gay activists alike to spot the substitution—and to take Hallmark to task for it. Gay activists claimed that Hallmark was catering to the powerful homophobic-Christmas-ornament buying group. Traditionalists wanted "gay" restored because … well, dag nab it, ya just don't monkey with Christmas. Let's see if a quick glance through Hallmark's 2013 "Dream Book of Christmas Ornaments" supports their case.

In the Dream Book you'll find the traditional "Toga Toga Toga" ornament, depicting the late John Belushi as Bluto Blutarsky from the movie "Animal House." You'll recall that "Animal House" helped to preserve the old wassailing tradition of drunken debauchery. A few pages later you'll find that jolly Christmas elf, The Joker, as portrayed by the late Heath Ledger in "The Dark Knight." Here's Hallmark's description of the ornament:

With a frighteningly malevolent appearance and a twisted twinkle in his eyes, The Joker dealt a hand of evil to the citizens of Gotham City—and to their protector—Batman. Despite his trademark grin, the taunts and tricks this madman has up his sleeve are definitely no laughing matter. Press the button to hear some of The Joker's most memorable lines.

Holy irony, Batman! Nothing like the glow of Gotham in flames to give you that warm yuletide feeling!

Hallmark didn't help its case by issuing a pseudo apology for tampering with the lyrics: "When the lyrics to 'Deck the Halls' were translated from Gaelic and published in English back in the 1800s," the company said in a statement, "the word 'gay' meant festive or merry. Today it has multiple meanings, which we thought could leave our intent open to misinterpretation."

I'm not for tailoring language to avoid perceived offense. In today's world, there's a better than even chance that anything you say will offend someone. Proof of that exists in a statement, made by Peter LaBarbera of the Chicago-based Americans for Truth About Homosexuality, in response to Hallmark lyric-tampering.

"Who could blame Hallmark for changing the Christmas carol … because homosexual activists stole the word 'gay,' " LaBarbera said.* "It used to mean 'happy' and 'joyful'—and now it means, basically, identifying a sexual perversion: homosexuality."

As that ol' Christmas elf The Joker himself might say, "Why so serious, Peter?"

Homosexuals haven't co-opted the word "gay."** "The Gay Nineties" needn't now be called "The Fun Nineties." The 1934 musical comedy "The Gay Divorcee," starring Fred Astaire and Ginger Rogers, has no hidden lesbian agenda. Like it or not, the English language allows words to carry more than one connotation. It's up to us to decide which one to use.

And that's the straight dope.

*The reasoning in LaBarbera's statement reminds me of "Homer's Phobia," an episode of "The Simpsons" in which Homer thinks Bart is "turning gay," so tries to take him to events he perceives as manly. Noted playwright, author and actor John Waters—who is openly gay—appears in the episode. At one point, the following dialog occurs:

John: Homer, what have you got against gays?
Homer: You know, it's not...usual! If there was a law, it would be against it!
Marge: Oh, please, Homer, you're embarrassing yourself!
Homer: No, they're embarrassing me! They're embarrassing America! They turned the Navy into a floating joke. They took our best names, like Bruce, Lance, and Julian. Those used to be our toughest, manliest names, but now they're just...
John: Queer?
Homer: And that's another thing; I resent you people using that word. That's our word for making fun of you! We need it!

**Editor's note: If you're an English major, you're probably aching to point out that in the late 14th century, one meaning of "gay" was "wanton or lascivious." By the 1890s, "gay" was a euphemism for prostitution; a "gay house" was a brothel. And if you're an English major, you've probably been parsing sentences such as "Would you like to super-size your drink?" since you earned your sheepskin.

There Is Nothing Like a ~~Dame~~ ~~Babe~~ ~~Girl~~ ~~Woman~~ Person

Author's note: This column first appeared in 2015.

I was for gender equality long before women made it a cause cèlébre in the Sixties. Growing up in a household in which the father didn't carry a house key because the mother couldn't drive—and thus was bound to be home at whatever hour he chose to sashay though the portal—probably had something to do with it.

Yet, even though women have made substantial strides toward true equality with men over the last 50 years, they still are paid less than men when holding down jobs of equal status. And, covertly or overtly, women may be refused opportunities simply because they were behind the door in heaven when penises were passed out. That's because gender bias is subtly pervasive.

For example, on August 10 retail giant Target announced that its stores would no longer use "gender-based" signage after a mother of three tweeted a photo of a Target sign that listed "Building Sets" and, below it, a separate sign for "Girls' Building Sets."

Exactly why this led to the mother's outrage is anyone's guess. Maybe her father also didn't carry a house key. The bigger problem is that she took to Twitter to vent her anger. Her need to emote publicly illustrates precisely how social media has enabled each of us to fall into his own personal Slough of Despond at even the slightest perceived insult.

But you can also blame her reaction on male-female stereotyping, which continue to plague us 50 years after the women's lib movement began. And stereotyping knows no gender.

In a recent study, researchers showed women two pictures of the same identically dressed man, one in which he leaned on a pickup truck, the other in which the vehicle was a subcompact sedan. Nine out of 10 women perceived the man in front of the truck as "sexier" and "manlier."

Men do no better. Put a woman executive in a power suit and male employees run screaming from her. Deck out the same woman in a short, tight skirt, 4-inch heels and a low-cut blouse, and men run after her like pigs to the slop trough.

I do, however, rather agree that gender-based signage should be unnecessary. If as an adult you can't pick a suitable toy for a child, you simply don't know the child well enough. Neither should it be necessary for bookstores to make suggestions for Mother's Day and Father's Day gifts based on the sex of the recipient. It's OK to buy a cookbook for Dad, or to get Mom lessons on how to field-strip her AK-47.

Bad Target! Putting up signs suggesting that boys and girls can't use the same building sets is a little like putting watermelon, collard greens and chitterlings in a "Food for Blacks" aisle in your food section.

I know it's tricky, but understand that women and men, although very different, are equally capable. In fact, I always tell females who don't really know me that I have always believed that women in power can screw up things just as badly as men.

Always gets a rise.

Dames are so emotional!

Tempest in a D Cup

Author's note: This column first appeared on February 13, 2013. I made one small addition for this book because I no longer have to worry about being "family friendly." See if you can spot it!

In choosing a topic for this week's column, I found several noteworthy events, all revolving around a common theme.
• On February 7, it was revealed that the powers that be at Mt. Lebanon Public Library had decided that a photograph of a mural showing an exposed female breast, part of an exhibit by photographer John Flatz, might cause small children to snicker, grown men to leer and grown women to have a sudden attack of the vapors. So they asked Flatz to replace the photo. He declined, choosing instead to cover the offending pectoral protruberance with a picture of a bra, along with an arrow pointing to it saying, "Censored by the Mt. Lebanon Public Library." Looks as if those who decide what offends in Lebo have been spending too much time watching the PBS series "Downton Abbey" and believe we are living in the 1920s. Egad, Jeeves! What's next? Exposed female ankles?

Library spokesmen say the ban is not censorship. That's good, because the Bible, also available in libraries, contains not only nudity, but also mass murder. And there's all that begatting. Where does censorship stop?

• Coincidentally, February 9 marked the 49th anniversary of the Beatles' first appearance on "The Ed Sullivan Show." Say what you like about the Fab Four, but they were undeniably cheeky. Maybe they need to play the Beatles at Lebo's library. After all, music hath charms to sooth the savage breast. NOTE: Avoid John Lennon's "Girl," in which Paul McCartney and George Harrison sing, "tit, tit, tit, tit."

• Tomorrow is Valentine's Day, a holiday usually involving the giving of flowers and candy to a loved one or, perhaps, an intimate, candlelit dinner involving something other than a footlong and curly fries at Sonic. But how many know the origins of St. Valentine's Day? And if they did, would they be offended?

Like many Christian festivals, St. Valentine's Day began as an effort by the Catholic Church to stop its members from celebrating pagan festivals, in this case Lupercalia, observed around Feb. 15. The Roman historian Plutarch described Lupercalia thusly: *At this time many of the noble youths and some of the magistrates run up and down through the city naked, for sport and laughter striking those they meet with shaggy thongs. And many women of rank also purposely get in their way, and like children at school present their hands to be struck, believing that the pregnant will thus be helped in delivery, and the barren to pregnancy.*

If you're thinking this sounds a lot like Beyonce's February 3 Super Bowl show, you're not alone.

The modern-day Plutarch—Wikipedia—adds that Lupercalia was celebrated "partly in honor of Lupa, the she-wolf who suckled the infant orphans, Romulus and Remus," who founded Rome.

Maybe Lebo's library planned a display on the history of St. Valentine's Day, but demurred, being unable to find a multi-cupped bra to cover the picture of Lupa suckling her adopted sons.

I guess that will remain one of Victoria's secrets.

Pack a Piece for Peace

As a writer, comic, and movie maker (we'll leave his private life out of this), Woody Allen is admirable. In "Take the Money and Run," his attempt to rob a bank is foiled when tellers debate whether his scrawled note reads, "I have a gun" or "I have a gub." And in the short-lived, hilarious TV show, "Police Squad," Leslie Nielsen karate-kicks away the guns from a pair of criminals, but they keep coming back with more weapons. "Look out! He's got a knife!" shrieks the comely bystander. "Look out! He's got a club! Look out! He's got a signed Picasso!" Dave was exposed at a formative stage to these and many more bizarre looks (think "Dr. Strangelove") at the wonderful world of weaponry. That's the only theory that begins to explain his take on arms and the man.

Stoopid Iz Az Stoopid Duz

I routinely look for news about stupid people. I admit that I sometimes do this to make myself feel better after I myself have done something dumb. Something like forgetting to put on an oven mitt before taking a baked dish out of the oven. Which I did a few years ago.

It is fascinating, in retrospect, to realize how long it took my brain to associate the sensation of extreme heat in my right hand with the 350-degree piece of metal it was holding. It took several seconds, I think. Then, reflex took over and the entrée became flying frittata. I survived, unscarred, and a better man for it. I figure it was God's way of giving me a little taste of how Hell might feel. At least at dinnertime.

Although I didn't do anything very dumb this weekend, on Monday I still went looking for people more stupid than I. And they were easy to find.

Take, for example, a Memphis father and son who, after discovering a takeout chicken place had given them the wrong order, went back to set things right—toting an AK-47.

Antonius Hart Sr. and Antonius Hart Jr. returned to Pirtle's

Chicken after discovering the cashier had not given them the order of wings they had requested. Told of the mistake, the cashier offered to make good, but Hart Sr. demanded extra wings because they had been forced to return to the restaurant. When the cashier refused, Hart revealed the assault rifle.

Another employee spotted the gun and called police, who charged Hart Sr. with aggravated assault and his son with facilitation of a felony. Seems pretty harebrained, I admit. But at least one customer interviewed by a local TV station about the incident thought it might improve customer service. I can't help but think that the Harts may have set the whole thing up.

The NRA will deny it, of course, but I think it was a vast, right-wings conspiracy.

Until the Harts nailed down the Dumb Clucks trophy, it looked like Sgt. Scott Biumi was a lock for the award. On April 18, Biumi, a 20-year veteran of the Dekalb, Georgia, police force, became tired of waiting in line at a McDonald's drive-thru window. So he hopped out of his car, walked to the front of the queue and yelled at Ryan Mash, the 18-year-old driver of car at the takeout window.

"Stop holding up the drive-thru line!" Biumi allegedly shouted. Mash apologized, but Biumi apparently felt Mash's reply was sarcastic. So he did the American thing.

He pulled a handgun, placed it against Mash's neck, and shouted, "You don't know who you're fuckin' with!"

The restaurant's security camera captured the entire incident, and witnesses wrote down the license plate number of the car Biumi was driving. Police traced the plate to his unmarked official car. Biumi's now on administrative leave and faces a court hearing in May. Let's hope the line's not too long.

The moral in all this?

Obviously, it's that fast food really can kill you. So eat at home.

The occasional glowing hand is worth it.

Support Your Local Samurai

Author's note: This column first appeared in January 2013, less than a month after National Rifle Association president Wayne La Pierre reacted to the Sandy Hook Elementary School shootings by lobbying for armed guards in schools, saying, "The only thing that stops a bad guy with gun is a good guy with gun."

2013 started off pretty well in the United States. It wasn't until 8 a.m. on January 1 that police encountered the first assault-weapon-toting wacko.

This occurred in San Jose, Calif., where officers responded to a report of a man armed with an assault weapon outside a residence. By the time police arrived, the suspect was nowhere in sight. But a description of his vehicle led them to a nearby transit station parking lot, where the suspect jumped out of his pickup truck, naked and brandishing a samurai sword.

"You're going to have to kill me," the suspect reportedly shouted at officers. They did not. I'll tell you why later.

I'd like to think that 2013 will bring less of the tragic news that has dominated media for the last decade. That won't be easy. Still, as much as we look forward with hope at the dawn of any new year, we also look back. So it figures that on New Year's Day I received an email from a friend who, like me, grew up in the 1950s—an email containing a PowerPoint presentation about "the good old days." It's loaded with references that, viewed through the gauze-filtered hindsight we all develop sometime in our 40s, cause us to think that those days were better.

For example, the presentation asks us to remember when "a quarter was a decent allowance." But it fails to ask us to also remember that the minimum wage in 1955 was 75 cents per hour. Today, with the minimum wage at $7.25 per hour, would you expect your kid to say that a weekly allowance of $2.42 is "decent?"

The PowerPoint also asks us to recall when "you'd reach into the muddy gutter for a penny." Quaint indeed. However, on New Year's Day I received a separate email from another friend, also raised in the '50s, who offered that she'd seen a penny in the street. Raised on the old saw, "See a penny, pick it up, all the day you'll have good luck," she stopped, removed her glove and bent to retrieve the penny—only to realize that she was in the middle of a crosswalk. Somehow, "... and you'll get run down by a truck" is not so catchy a finish to this rhyme.

As for the nude rude dude whose story began this column, the police did not have to kill him. This was because the National Samurai Sword Association (NSSA)—in a move no one anticipated—had stationed naked, samurai-sword-brandishing members at every transit station in California at midnight. Because we all know that the only thing that stops a naked, samurai-sword-brandishing bad guy is ...

I made that up. Police captured the swordsman after he ran, fell down and dropped the sword. Don't worry, you'll be able to see it all recreated on "Naked Samurai Island," premiering February 1 on E!

I made that up, too. At least I think I did.

It's only January 3, and the network sweeps haven't begun.

Home, Home and Deranged

When it comes to the tender feelings, Dave is more sed-imental than sentimental. Still, there are a few things that seem to make his heartstrings vibrate. Here are two from his history of growing up in Pittsburgh, a city that is passionate about its history as a steel center, a sports mecca and a melting pot where the huddled masses worked their way to freedom.

Things That Go Blink in the Night

Author's note: This column first appeared in 1995. Western Pennsylvanians older than 40 will remember the Alcoa sign that hung above the city on the side of Mt. Washington. It eventually became the Mobay sign, then the Bayer sign, then the Blue Cross sign, then an ugly mishmash of blank panels and, finally, the Sprint Mobile sign. As I write this in early 2017, Pittsburgh City Council is seeking to kick Sprint off the sign. Most of the places mentioned in this column are no longer here.

* * *

Night in the city looks pretty to me. – Joni Mitchell

If you've stared before sunset at the side of Mt. Washington, the sign looks sort of like a giant Band-Aid, stuck up there on the side of the hill to help heal some ancient wound. During the day, its dull white and gray panels are arranged in a mosaic that spells out "Pittsburgh." I know—as a landmark, HOLLYWOOD, it ain't.

But at night, ah ... at night. That's when the sign comes into its own, as what might be the world's largest digital watch flashes out, in red, the correct time and various public service announcements.

For 25 years, until the first of this year, these were followed, in blue, by the triangular logo of the Aluminum Company of America, immediately trailed by, again in red, five letters: A-L-C-O-A. It was a part of Pittsburgh, the Alcoa sign. But in December Alcoa informed Martin Advertising, owner of the sign, that renting the 65-foot by 222-foot electronic billboard was no longer a priority. The logo and company name of Miles, formerly Mobay Corp., will appear sometime this spring.

But even after it does, night in the city still will look pretty to me, although never quite as pretty as it did in 1962, when I first made it Downtown, with my dad.

We'd followed the nose of his black Rambler station wagon 30-odd miles southeast along Ohio River Boulevard from New Brighton, my hometown, and started across the Manchester Bridge[1] when I first spotted the sign. I'd never seen anything like it.

Oh, New Brighton had a clock/sign—a thin, floodlit strip that overlooked the borough from a hillside in Beaver Falls, across the Beaver River. But that sign had a keystone-shaped clock with hands. "Time to Buy Keystone Bread," it read in 1962, advertising a local bakery. Madison Avenue ala Beaver Valley. The Big Apple come west. The Big Appalachian?

But Keystone's bread and butter couldn't compare to the sign on Mt. Washington. I was awestruck by it, and by other things that went blink in the night.

The Flame Steakhouse[2], for one, situated where Liberty and Fifth avenues join at the rib. "The Flame," too, was spelled out in giant neon letters. Inside, a man wearing a real chef's hat grilled steaks over tongues of flame that licked ceilingward in almost the same way their fiery cousins had shot toward the night sky from Jones and Laughlin's Aliquippa steel plant[3], which we'd passed as we motored toward the city.

90

I'd never seen a real chef in person. Come to think of it, I'd never seen a real steak. Mom is a graduate of that school of cooking that requires her to pound a cheap cut of beef with the three serated blades of a meat hatchet before she drags it through flour and pan-fries it.

A little further up Fifth Avenue we encountered the Warner Theater[4], our destination. Its marquee sparkled. Dressed in suits, small-towners in the big city, Dad and I had come to see "The Wonderful World of the Brothers Grimm" in Cinerama. But we were early, so kept walking—something you could do at night in the city then without worrying about being mugged, drugged or hugged.

We strolled up Fifth to Smithfield, turned right, then turned right again on Forbes. Blam! The lights of the Casino burlesque house[5] assaulted my eyes.

"That's where the girls are," said Dad, a man of extremely few words and even fewer women. He offered no further explanation. He knew; I knew. He knew I knew.

We'd made the circuit to Fifth again before I caught sight of the Gulf Building[6], its pyramidal top red and flashing. Now once again bathed in white as it originally was in the Thirties, the pinnacle of the Gulf Building fits right in with the modern skyscrapers at Fifth Avenue Place and Oxford Centre. But to me, the Gulf Building's top is lifeless now. Better red than dead.

Finally, Dad and I watched our movie in a theater that soon would be converted to a mini-mall, only blocks from a strip joint that soon would fall victim to the wrecker's ball, then walked under the winking eye of the Gulf Building, which soon would go nearly black, past a steakhouse that eventually would become an electronics store and drove home past a steel mill whose open-hearth furnaces soon would be banked.

To me, the Alcoa sign represents innocence. Probably because when I first saw it, the biggest decision facing me each morning was which pair of black socks to wear to school.

91

True, the sign no longer says A-L-C-O-A. But at least it still blinks.

Only its name has been changed to protect my innocence.

[1] *The Manchester Bridge crossed the Allegheny River from Pittsburgh's North Side to the Point. It was replaced in 1969 by the Fort Duquesne Bridge.*

[2] *A small park now occupies the former site of The Flame.*

[3] *The last remnants of the Jones & Laughlin Steel Corp. in Aliquippa were scoured away by salvagers in 2010.*

[4] *The Warner Theater, once a movie palace in the grand style, was transformed into a shopping mall in the 1980s. The building is no longer occupied.*

[5] *The Casino Theater burlesque house was demolished in 1965.*

[6] *The Gulf Building (now the Gulf Tower) still stands. Its illuminated pyramidal top has undergone many incarnations, the latest as a color-coded weather beacon for Pittsburgh's KDKA-TV.*

After the Ball Was Over

Sixth grade, 1960, Central Elementary School, New Brighton, Pa.
That's chubby me, surrounded by girls, in the second row.

The wall is gone now, and so is Central School. But I remember both, mostly for different reasons. Memories blend though, on an early fall afternoon 30 years ago.

We are in our 40s now, the 35 sixth-graders who in October 1960 were one month into our final 180 days as classmates. In September 1955, substantially the same group had entered the first-grade classroom at Central, an ancient, three-story brown brick building where many of our parents had attended high school. Junior high soon would scatter our little circle as an agate does a group of marbles.

My classmates and I already shared many marvels: cursive writing; the replacement of inkwells with ballpoint pens; Elvis. And before 1960 ended, we would acquire more memories—of Kennedy and Nixon; of classmates such as Timmy, who because he saw himself as The World's Fastest Talker slurred his lines in our Christmas play, Dickens' "A Christmas Carol," so badly that they sounded like this: IAMTHEGHOSTOFCHRISTMASPAST. Of Billy, who in 1961 would become The Boy Puberty Forgot. Yes, when I was 11, it was a very good year.

Yet most of these tales out of school were at recess until people began comparing the Pirates' pennant race of 1990 to that of 1960. Then they came marching back to my sixth-grade classroom.

And leading the melancholy parade was a crewcut young man

wearing a baggy flannel outfit with the number 9 stitched to its back.

His name is Bill Mazeroski.

And he is why I—and many more people, both older and younger— paused Saturday to remember October 13, 1960.

My classmates and I didn't leave school at 3:30 as usual that afternoon.

Baseball card pose, 1960

We remained at our desks, listening intently to a battery-powered transistor radio tuned to the seventh game of a World Series in which the New York Yankees and the Pittsburgh Pirates each had won three games. The radio belonged to Central's janitor, Mr. Barr. He'd lent it to us.

"Here," he said, dressed in institutional greens, clutching his chest as he handed over the radio, a custodian surrendering custody. "It's too much for me." With good reason.

Nines were wild that day. Moments before, Pittsburgh catcher Hal Smith had given the Bucs a 9-7 lead in the eighth. But the Yankees had drawn even in the top of the ninth. Now the teams were tied at nine, heading into the bottom of the ninth. And No. 9 was at the plate.

As all true Pirates fans well know, Ralph Terry's first pitch to

Maz was a ball. The second was also a ball: a ball heading over the ivy-covered left field wall of Forbes Field.[*]

I can still hear the shout of joy that burst simultaneously from 35 throats. It brought a teacher rushing from her classroom next door.

"What happened?" she asked.

"MAZEROSKI HIT A HOME RUN!" we screamed, en masse.

"What?" she asked, unable to decipher our 120-decible shout.

"MAZ HIT A HOMER!" we screamed again, leaping from our seats and hugging each other.

"Oh, is that all?" she said. And left the room. I hated fifth grade.

But I will always love Mr. Barr. Without his sacrificial act, I would have no firsthand memory of Maz's mighty blast.

Yes, I've seen the film thousands of times—Maz skipping around second base, waving his hat, being mobbed by fans and teammates at home plate. It's not the same. When someone mentions The Homer, it's Room 6 at Central I think of first.

Thanks Mr. Barr. Sorry I took so long to say it. Were it not for your weak heart, I would remember you only as a kindly, bespectacled old man who brought a bucket of green sawdust each time a classmate threw up. But last Saturday, you made me 11 again.

The wall is gone now, and so is Central School. But I remember.

Editor's note: Forbes Field, torn down in 1970 as part of the expansion of the University of Pittsburgh, enjoys the status of a vanished cathedral in the hearts of Pittsburgh sports fans. It showcased the unique talents of the remarkable Roberto Clemente, who could rifle a baseball from the right-field warning track straight into home plate—no cut-off man. Roberto won the Gold Glove for 12 consecutive seasons and batted over .300 in 13 seasons. His heart matched his talent; he died in an airplane accident, en route to deliver aid to earthquake victims in Nicaragua in 1972. Pittsburghers remember him with respect and affection and measure every athlete against the professional and personal standards he set. A statue of Clemente outside PNC Park reminds us all of the gift he was to our city and to major league baseball.

A Paid Political Announcement

It's hard to pigeonhole Dave's political beliefs. He might best be understood as one who is so very far to the left that he's done a 180 and landed near the right on at least some issues. Mostly, he's exasperated by the lack of common sense that permeates our current political landscape—that, and a pretentiousness that won't permit folks to laugh at themselves or their political positions.

Blinded by the Light

Author's note: From time to time I adopt the persona of the True Patriot aroused to Righteous Anger by some perceived affront. I am happy to say that sometimes, people think I'm serious.

Patriots:
I want to talk to you today about a new socialist threat to America: compact fluorescent light bulbs (CFLs).

To prove to you that CFLs are, indeed, socialist-inspired, I need point out only two things. First, in 2007 the Russian government began urging its citizens to buy CFLs to save energy—energy that they surely have channeled into thermonuclear devices aimed at the United States. Since when does the U.S. do what Commies do? Other than invade Afghanistan, that is. Second—and this is so obvious that I'm sure you've already figured it out for yourself— both "communist" and "compact" begin with C-O-M.

Perhaps, like me, you have already fallen victim to Creeping Flourescentism, replacing your incandescent bulbs with CFLs because the Godless Liberals in Congress brainwashed us into thinking that saving energy is good for the future of our children.

But I ask you: Did we worry about saving energy in WWII? Or during the Cold War? No, we slurped up all the energy we could, igniting it to blind the Enemies of Freedom with the sheer incandescent brilliance of the Statue of Liberty's Torch. But now these light-sucking "Black Hole Liberals" want to make Lady Liberty's afterglow an afterthought. Here's how.

The misleadingly titled "Energy Independence and Security Act of 2007" calls for a 25-percent increase in energy efficiency for light bulbs, to be phased in between 2012 and 2014, beginning with our beloved 100-watt bulbs and eventually attacking 40-watters. Proponents of this law have tried to sway you and me by pointing out that no one is required to use CFLs, that the new bulbs give off just as much light, use less energy, last longer and cost less over the life of the bulb than incandescents. But I say this: If CFLs are so much better, why didn't Thomas Edison invent *them*?

The 100-watt incandescent bulb holds a place of honor in America. For example, it is the glowing heart of Hasbro's Easy Bake Oven. I, for one, do not want to eat cookies lovingly prepared by prepubescent girls in an oven using a socialist power source. And 100-watt incandescent bulbs are absolutely the best for drying marijuana seeds. Or so some liberals have told me.

God meant for Americans to have our homes illuminated instantly at the flip of a switch, not for us to stumble around for several seconds trying to find our handguns while CFLs warm up. So I'm calling on all True Patriots to follow the lead of Republican Representatives Joe Barton of Texas and Michelle Bachman of Minnesota, who each have sponsored bills to reverse this dimwitted law. Begin hoarding 100-watt incandescent bulbs. Then throw them at the jackbooted federals when they come for you.

They told us how much water we can use to flush our toilets. They told us our cars had to get better mileage. Let this CFL power play stand, and soon they will take away our God-given right to keep meat in an icebox rather than in a refrigerator.

Americans, face the flag and repeat after me: *I will give up my incandescents when they unscrew them from my cold, dead sockets.*

Setting the Record Straight

Author's note: This column first appeared in July 2016 after Donald Trump's campaign tried to downplay the use of a six-pointed star and images of money in an attack ad against Hillary Clinton. Overlooking the long-standing stereotypical linking of Jews with money, Trump claimed the star was not a Star of David but, rather, a six-pointed sheriff's star.

My fellow Americans:

The joyous sounds of the celebration of freedom still reverberate from the purple mountains and echo across the fruited plains. So it pains me that I must address the so-called controversy invented by the dishonest media concerning my backyard Independence Day fireworks display.

I refuse to apologize to anyone who thought that the six-pointed stars that burst so joyously in the heavens were Stars of David, and thus anti-Semitic. They were, rather, Stars of Andy.

Specifically, Andy Taylor, who wore just such a star while proudly serving his country as sheriff of Mayberry, North Carolina, in the 1960s. What a great American tradition, the sheriff! Really.

Unfortunately, several calls to Sheriff Taylor to obtain his personal verification of this fact went straight to voicemail, my chief of staff assures me. But no doubt Andy and Deputy Barney Fife are enjoying retirement as part of the Mayberry Militia, patrolling the streets of Mayberry to ensure that radical Islamic terrorists never infiltrate our borders through what has to be in the top 1 percent of our greatest states. Maybe the top 5 percent. But right up there, believe me. And let me point out that archival footage of Sheriff Taylor is readily available on YouTube.

Next, to address the rumors about the uniforms of my security team. Many in the devious, twisted media have said these white sheets reminded them of those worn by members of the Ku Klux Klan. But I must honestly tell you that they were meant as a tribute to my great friend John Landis—great, great American—and his classic film about the superiority of the American collegiate education system, "Animal House."

What could be more typically American? After a hard week's study designed to raise our great nation once again to the pinnacle of worldwide business, our young men and women enjoy a great time at a fraternity mixer! I mean, when I say "toga," don't you say "party?" Of course you do! And that's what we had in mind when we had those uniforms made. American-made, believe me! And, hands down, we make the best sheets. At least 500-thread count, I can personally vouch for that. Available in the souvenir shop.

And, lest I forget: The "towel head" portable toilets we provided were not, as suggested by so many reporters—who were admitted free to the fireworks, I might add—a disparaging reference to those of Middle Eastern descent. They were but a patriotic reference to the term "head" as used by our brave fighting men and women in the U.S. Navy. And we spared no expense, so we provided towels. Real, cotton towels. Made from real, American-grown cotton. Ask any of the real, American washroom attendants who handed them out.

Finally, I want to assure you that the burning dummies surrounding the fireworks launching area were not, as some in the lying media have claimed, depictions of illegal Mexican immigrants thwarted from entering our great country. They were, in fact, a tribute to the 1960 John Sturges film, "The Magnificent Seven." As I'm sure you all know, that amazing, amazing epic, based on a true story, recounted how seven American Special Forces members became trapped behind enemy lines while attempting to build a wall between Texas and Mexico. The movie's star, my longtime friend Yul Brynner—a truly great American—confirmed this last night during what my chief of staff assures me was a long email exchange.

But I can't deny that the dummies were, in fact, meant to depict the lying, raping, murdering, four-wheeling, drug-dealing, job-stealing foreign banditos who in the movie were dispatched so efficiently by our brave fighting men—all using U.S.-made revolvers and rifles that some say Americans shouldn't be allowed to own. Maybe some of the banditos were Mexican—I don't know. If they were, I assume some were good people. But probably at least half of them were Mexicans. Bad Mexicans.

We're looking into that, and we'll have a white paper for you in the morning.

Revolution for Dummies

Author's note: This column first appeared in 2015.

With their January 2 armed occupation of the Malheur National Wildlife Refuge in Oregon's high desert country, Ammon Bundy and his followers have given revolutionaries a bad name. Initially appearing to be a group of rugged individualists seeking to protest "land grabbing" by the federal government, the group last week succeeded in portraying its members as a bunch of namby-pambys.

A former member of the group told *The Oregonian* newspaper that Bundy and compatriot Ryan Lane, a militia leader from Montana, had begun to organize the occupation months previously. But the group seems to have been woefully unprepared for the long-term siege they claimed to be willing to endure. One week after the occupation began, Bundy's mother released to social media a wishlist of supplies that her son and his followers had neglected to pack in their haste to be modern-day Minutemen. It was a list that would have made any true revolutionary retch.

Included among the "necessities" they requested are:
- Sliced cheese (because cutting through a block of longhorn would dull your Navy SEALS knife)
- Razors (even though every true revolutionary has a beard)
- French Vanilla creamer

Moreover, if your revolutionaries require *menthol* cigarettes, hair conditioner, oven cleaner, hamburgers, hot dogs *and* bratwurst—and demand both mayonnaise *and* Miracle Whip—don't ask me to consider them rugged.

The list also has a number of spelling errors that make me think that Ammon family members skipped not only American history classes but also English. If you can't spell apron, ("apran"), ice scraper ("scrapper") or shaving cream ("crème"), don't ask for my support.

How depressing. What would America look like today had some of our most famous revolutionaries been of the Bundys' ilk?

1777-1778: During the long winter at Valley Forge, General George Washington writes to his wife, Martha:

You say the children ask how cold it is here at Valley Forge. Well, simply tell them that the men in rank say that the temperature gives a whole new meaning to "freeze your privates." (There is levity even in war, my love; chastise me not.) Meanwhile, we struggle to endure, with too few blankets and shoes, and although the men say they find tree bark quite palatable, I fear that mutiny is afoot and our cause is lost unless you can convince Dolly Madison to send some of her famous snack cakes.

1836: Excerpt from a note found in the rubble of the Alamo, passed down over generations and brought for valuation to "The Antiques Roadshow":

Who knows where Bowie is? Last I seen him, he had put a gingham apran on a cactus and was carrying 'her' toward the barracks. Tell everyone things is dire. We has plenty of hardtack, but Crockett and his boys say that unless they gets some mild salsa, they's going over the wall tonight. So send some of that along with the tequila and churros we ast fer yestiddy. And more sopapillas, too; we are but mortal men.—Travis

Sliced cheese? Downright revolting!

Sometimes You Get the Bear ...

Today's cautionary tale comes courtesy of the Pennsylvania Game Commission.

In November 2009, Charles W. Olsen Jr. of Wilkes-Barre was arrested after trying to claim as a legitimate hunting kill a 707-pound black bear he had shot after luring the hapless animal to a killing zone using doughnuts and other sweets laid out in the woods. Of the 28 states that allow bear hunting, Pennsylvania is one of 18 in which bear baiting is illegal.

At first I thought that BCSI (Bear Crime Scene Investigation) personnel might have been clued to Olsen's methods by the thin coating of powdered sugar on the bear's upper lip and the Starbucks grandé chai tea latte they had to pry from its cold, dead paws.

But here's the real story: Olsen confessed to the crime only after a Pennsylvania wildlife conservation officer, who had spotted Olsen driving a pastry-filled truck a week before bear season, alerted those in charge of checking bear kills.

Spare me protests about how this is just one more example of the Obama administration's secret plan to deprive us of our Constitutional right to drive confection-filled vehicles.

Now, I'm willing to consider that there may have been extenuating circumstances. Perhaps as a child Olsen was traumatized by the Grimm treatment of Goldilocks by the Three Bears, although in my view the bears were victims of a home invasion.

But even when legal, bear baiting certainly doesn't qualify as "hunting." Where's the chase, the challenge, the matching of wits with a wily opponent that so many cite as their reasons for hunting?

Yet bear baiting has its defenders. In 2002 Rick Posig, then president of the Wisconsin Bear Hunters Association, tried to explain to the Milwaukee *Sentinel* that bear baiting isn't as easy as it sounds: "You can sit on a bait for hours on end," Posig said. "The bears are smart. They know when you're there and when you're not there."

In other words, bear baiters are not smarter than the average bear. So they cheat. And sitting is very, very hard work.

Here's bear baiting in a nutshell: You lure bears to a killing zone using beaver carcasses hung in the trees, or bags of crème-filled cookies, or cooking grease poured around the base of a 50-gallon drum filled with rotting fish and chained to a tree—all baiting tips detailed in "A Black Bear Baiting Guide" on BigGameHunt.net.

And then you kill them. For "sport."

I never thought I'd be quoting ex-wrestler (and former Minnesota governor) Jesse Ventura as a voice of reason, but here goes. In 2003, discussing his opposition to bear baiting, Ventura said: "Going out there and putting jelly doughnuts down, and Yogi comes up and sits there and thinks he's found the mother lode for five days in a row—and then you back-shoot him from a tree? That ain't sport. That's an assassination."

On April 29, Olsen was found guilty of breaking several Pennsylvania game laws and fined $6,800 plus court costs. He likely will lose his hunting and trapping privileges for three years.

… and sometimes the bear gets you.

I wish there could be some kind of community service involved —cleaning bear dens at a zoo for a couple years, maybe.

That's what I'd call just desserts.

God Bless Us, Every One

Dave's friends always stand behind him—far behind him in anticipation of a righteous lightning bolt. Many see his insistence that key religious figures were, at one point, actually human as irreverence. But anyone who believes a Divine Being created the dachshund also believes in a Divine sense of humor.

A Guide for the Married Savior

Author's note: This column first appeared in 2015, after a scrap of papyrus obtained from an unknown collector was found to contain the phrase, "Jesus said to them, 'My wife ...'." The so-called "Gospel of Jesus' Wife" gave rise to speculation that Christ may have been married.

My first mistake, Peter thought, was making this a dinner meeting.

"People! People!" he called out, rather miffed. "Gather 'round, please! Luke, I think you've had enough of the little meatballs. Everybody, grab a slab of floor so we can wrap this thing up before midnight."

The other 11 men, some grumbling a bit, came forward and, after much shuffling of feet, settled in.

"Mark, will you please read the minutes of the last meeting?"

"It was Luke's turn to take them," Mark said defensively.

Peter wrinkled his brow and let out a long sigh.

"Oh, for ... Luke?"

111

"I thought Matthew was doing them," Luke said, not looking up.

"Matthew?"

"Pretty sure John has, 'em," Matthew replied.

"John?"

"No one told me to take them until about halfway through the meeting," John replied.

Peter scowled and pinched the bridge of his nose. "Look ... why don't you all write down what you think happened last time, then maybe we can pull one version together when we have some free time."

"Sounds like a plan!" Luke said, high-fiving Mark.

Peter shook his head. "Moving on ... Bartholomew? PR report?"

"We have a potential situation," Bartholomew said.

"Such as?" Peter asked.

"Such as this thing about Jesus' better half," Bartholomew said, standing up and placing his hands on his hips.

"Hey! We agreed not to talk about her!" shouted Thaddeus.

"So we did," Bartholomew countered, "but someone apparently forgot to tell Jesus."

"What did he say this time?" Peter asked wearily.

"It started out the same as all the rest. Some Pharisees confronted him about the usual stuff. You know how he likes to rile them up. So ... well ... he told them he's married."

All eyes turned toward Peter, who was now staring at the floor. "And this helps us how?" he asked.

"Well," Simon offered, "at least we won't have to deal with the gay rumors anymore."

"That's not a plus in my view," said Peter, clearly at the limit of his patience.

"It doesn't help," said Bartholomew. "But what really hurts is that we'd done such a good job of hiding her from the media 'til now. Always a separate room and a different name at the inns. But we'll handle it."

"I can't wait to hear how," said Judas.

"We tell them it was a parable," Bartholomew said flatly. "That always works. They still haven't figured out the 'I am the door' thing."

"I say we just deny he ever said it," said Andrew. "Were there any scribes lurking?"

"Not that I know of," said Bartholomew. "But that's what I thought last time. Then scraps of papyrus start cropping up in caves. The parable thing is the way to go. Trust me"

"Pardon me," said Thomas, "but aren't you the one who said that robes with I'M WITH JESUS embroidered on them would sell like matzo at Passover?"

"Natural market fluctuation," said Bartholomew, turning his palms up and shrugging.

"I don't know why we're all so worried about this," said Philip. "Is there any among us who doesn't agree that since he got married, Jesus has been a much different man? A better man? It seems to have anchored him. I say she's been a steadying influence."

The others nodded their agreement.

"Well, then ... Boss?" Bartholomew asked.

Peter closed his eyes again, then opened them and looked Heavenward. He clasped his hands together and stood.

"Gentlemen, we do nothing," he said. "No matter what Jesus says or is supposed to have said, people ultimately will judge him by his body of work. They'll either believe, or they won't." He sat down. "We do nothing. Can I have a motion to that effect?"

"I so move," said Philip.

"Seconded," said James the Younger.

"All those in favor?" said Peter. Twelve hands shot up.

"It's unanimous, then," said Peter. "This meeting is adjourned."

Halfway down the stairs, James the Younger caught Peter's elbow. He smiled. "You handled that like a real pro."

"Thanks, kid!" said Peter. "But—just between you and me—the world's going to end soon anyway. It's not like, 2,000 years from now, anyone's going to be arguing over whether Jesus was married."

Just Say Noah

Author's note: This column appeared in 2015 after I read about plans to build Ark Encounter, a full-size replica of Noah's Ark, as part of an Old Testament theme park in Kentucky. It's written from the point of view of someone who takes the Bible literally and, in my experience, often misquotes scripture attempting to prove a point. A multi-million dollar Ark is fine—it's your money. But would it not be better to spend its $48 million projected cost to help those in need here and now rather than ask these same people to shell out $60 each to see a recreation of something that may or may not have happened before Christianity was invented? Apparently not: Ark Encounter opened in July 2016.

You'll have to get in line behind me to see Ark Encounter if it opens as planned in Kentucky. I'm really looking forward to seeing how Noah managed to build a three-level, 500-foot-long wooden boat at least 5,900 years before the first Home Depot opened. At the age of 600. Without Craftsman power tools. But it's in the Bible, so I believe he did. Ark Encounter is being planned by the good folks who erected Creation World not too long ago—also in Kentucky. So, John Denver, you were wrong when you sang that West Virginia is "almost Heaven."

I was one of the 400,000 folks who visited the Creation Museum in 2007, when it opened. It does a real spiffy job of explaining that Earth is only 6,000 years old and that God created it in just six, 24-hour days. They get a lot of flack from non-believers saying that these numbers are way off. But I'm here to tell you that God—being God—could do anything he wanted to do, in whatever period of time he wanted to do it. And since calendars and watches hadn't been invented yet, how can anyone be sure? Besides, God knew he had to be done in six days so people could make it to church on Sunday.

While I'm on the subject, I want to say that the folks who blessed us with the Creation Museum are also spot on when they depict dinosaurs and humans living at the same time. "Scientists" tell us this isn't so, but here is a little tidbit I'll bet you didn't know: No way would the God-fearing executives at network TV have let Hanna-Barbera get away with "The Flintstones" if there wasn't some grain of truth to it. (Well, foot-powered cars don't make too much sense to me, but then, neither does the Internet. It will all be revealed on the One Great Day.)

But back to Ark Encounter. No one at Tim's Discount Lumber Yard could tell me how long a cubit is, but somehow the master builders at the Creation Museum figured it out for themselves and are planning to construct an exact replica of Noah's mighty ship. Well, not quite exact because Tim doesn't know what kind of tree produces "gopher wood." But I'm willing to bet that Wolmanized lumber will be just as good, because God has a way of taking care of things like this. The new ark will have three decks—just like the original—and I hear there are plans to show how cagey old Noah, using the technology of the times, could squeeze in two of every animal and invent a system to remove all that animal waste and ventilate the ship. (Princess Cruises could use that!)

I also can't wait to see the First Century Village, the Tower of Babel and the 10 Plagues of Egypt ride that will accompany Ark Encounter. I wrote to Mike Zovath, co-founder and vice-president of

Ark Encounter, and suggested a "Hebrews of the Mediterranean" ride, but he hasn't responded.

I read the other day that although Ark Encounter has $12.3 million in donations with another $12.7 million in pledges, it will take $23 million more to actually get the Ark started. That's a lot of "shekels," to use the biblical term! So I voided my $50 check for Oklahoma tornado relief and rewrote one to Ark Encounter. It was an easy decision.

Do your part, that's what the Golden Rule says.

In Search of Chocolate Jesus

Gather round, children, and Unkie Dave will tell you a story while we trim the tree.

It were nigh unto 20 years ago when I began my Christmas quest. It was a dark time—pre-Google, in fact. Don't roll your eyes, Tiffany! That's right: pre-Google. If you wanted to look something up, you had to go to the library. L-I-B-R-A-R-Y, Lindsay. A place where they keep books. No, not Barnes and Noble, Austin.

Look—we'll never get this thing up if you don't stop asking questions. Hand me the Tree Dazzler, Nathan.

I was a newspaper reporter back then, kids. N-E-W-S-P-A-P-E-R. Yes, like the one that just went all digital, Rhiannon. Stop eating the popcorn, Shaquille! Where was I? Oh—the quest.

I wrote columns back then, kids, once a week. Much harder than twice a month, like these wimpy writers of today complain about. Always searching for new ideas, I was. And it occurred to me, while I was trimming my own Christmas tree—just like we are now—that I had never seen a chocolate Nativity set. You know—chocolate Wise Men, chocolate shepherds, chocolate Mary and

Joseph, holy infant so creamy and mild. Why? I wondered.

The simple reason, I figured, was that no one wanted to bite the head off Baby Jesus.

Yes, Robin! Ewwwww!

But I couldn't see why people thought that would be so icky. After all, we have no problem eating chocolate crosses at Easter time, right? I figured there had to be some biblical reason why people were so afraid.

Maybe the apostle Peter—part of Jesus' squad and a bit of an emo, they say—got mad at Jesus, and said something mean.

"Peter!" Jesus probably replied. "It's OK to kvetch, but you don't have to bite my head off!"

Yes, that's exactly what happened, Harrison!

As I was saying: I couldn't find a chocolate Nativity set anywhere. And I couldn't Google it to see if such a thing existed. Well known candy-makers manufactured everything out of chocolate: snowmen, Santas, reindeer—even a Stanley Cup! But no chocolate Jesus. Yes, Philomena. Awwwwwwww!

So I just gave up and wrote about something else Christmassy—a Black Friday stampede at Walmart, maybe. I don't remember.

Well, kids, time passed, and a new century arrived, and many good things came with it! All of you, for example! Before long, someone invented the Internet, and now we have streaming video and online shopping and fake news and blogs and the chance to digitally beat dead horses 24/7.

You'll understand when you're old enough to vote, Barack.

And, of course, now we have Google, so I asked Google—What? I have a flip phone, Kayla; I can't ask Siri.

And … guess what Google told me! That's right. Now we have chocolate Nativity sets! How many? Lots, Mateus! There's even one recommended by Oprah that has cherries in the middle! No, Polly, Dr. Oz hasn't recommended a healthy one yet.

Your moms and dads can buy candy molds so you can make your own! But if they're busy on Twitter, they can buy ready-to-eat ones. Those come in milk chocolate or white chocolate—just in case milk chocolate gives you a headache, or if you want to express your politics in a subtle way.

But ya know what? All the sets Unkie Dave saw have Mary holding her baby in her arms! So it's still going to be pretty tough to bite the head off Baby Jesus unless you're willing to take out two-thirds of the Holy Family.

Yes, I know that they make Nativity sets portraying Jesus as a duck, or an otter. And that they make Nativity sets out of bacon and cocktail wieners, and that no one seems afraid to eat those. Why? Some things even Google can't tell us, Billy Bob.

But let's finish the tree!

Hand me the "Make America Great Again" hat ornament, Tori.

What do you mean, it broke already?

Well … grab Hallmark's Mexican Snowman Feliz Navidad Musical Ornament instead.

Covering All the Bases

If we paid clergy as much as we pay baseball players, would we expect them to pray hurt?

This thought occurred to me when I realized some years ago that the start of baseball season and Easter often come within days of each other, and this year is no exception. And no matter what set of beliefs you may hold, you'll have to admit that Easter and Opening Day have lots in common.

For example, on both Opening Day and Easter, the seats of their respective arenas are clogged with people who come out only twice a year—to church on Easter and Christmas, to the ballpark on Opening Day and Closing Day. Most of the spectators on these days may grasp the basic rules of the game but probably need a roster to tell the players apart. This is particularly true in many of today's mega-churches, which have so many pastors and services that the clergy have to co-ordinate to make sure that the pastor in one service isn't forgiving a sin that the pastor in another service spent 25 minutes condemning.

I was about 6 years old and still dazzled by both baseball and church when I first noticed how much the two intertwine. The initial connection I made was obvious—Sunday's a big day for each. When I was 10, I found another parallel.

My family belonged to a denomination begat by Southern Baptists, and sermons routinely ran 45 minutes but sometimes went into extra innings. One Sunday, in the bottom of the 10th, it became obvious that the starting preacher was tiring. So they brought in a relief preacher. And he got the save—a man who bolted to the front of the sanctuary, knelt down and professed faith. "Church is just like baseball!" I thought. And nothing I've seen since then has shaken my faith in that observation.

In fact, about the only differences I've discovered between baseball and religion are that, in church, everyone roots for the home team, and churchgoers trying to get out of the parking lot are much surlier than baseball fans doing the same. These, and I've never seen a pew-clearing brawl.

I'll admit that most of this is only my opinion. So let me balance things by revealing what I learned about religion from the players themselves. I first ran my baseball-religion hypothesis past a friend who had a divinity degree but was working as a religion editor. I'd come up with some pretty interesting parallels, he allowed, yet he pointed out that even well-paid people of the cloth might only make about $80,000 a year. At the time, Major League Baseball's minimum yearly starting salary was $100,000. Strike one. But then he told me that in some cases, pastors seeking a new position are required to preach at a neutral church so the selection committee from the prospective new church will not be unduly influenced by the congregation of the old. Now, to me, that's a preachoff (playoff). Home run!

Not much later, I received final confirmation of my baseball-cum-religion theory from two Catholic priests I interviewed. After they had described the fulfilling aspects of their jobs, I asked them to outline a few of the hazards of being a priest.

"If we mess up," the younger priest told me, smiling, "the bishop will reassign us to New Castle*." In other words, the manager (bishop) will send us down (reassign) us to the minors (New

Castle.) And sure enough, the younger father did, in fact, find himself at a small parish outside New Castle a few years later. He's in AAA (Cranberry Township[1]) now.

Since then, I've been trying to determine which league (denomination) has correctly interpreted the ground rules. Raised a protestant, since coming of age I have attempted to cover all the bases by attending services in Methodist, Lutheran, Baptist, Catholic, Anglican and non-denominational churches and by studying Buddhism and other disciplines. That's because even with a program, all the players look about the same to me.

But the Catholics have the best uniforms.

New Castle is a city of about 20,000 some 50 miles northwest of Pittsburgh. As cities go, it is decidedly not major league.

[1] *Cranberry Township is an affluent northern suburb of Pittsburgh.*

Lightning Striking Again

Author's note: This column first appeared in 2010.

Religion, they say, is the opiate of the masses. Ah, if only religion—like opium—would put us into a stupor rather than make us think we are qualified to discern God's intentions. But it doesn't. So quite often some random event occurs that elicits, if not discussion, then commentary on the religious overtones of the incident. Take, for example, two things that happened on June 15.

First, lightning struck a BP tanker being used to store oil sucked up from a leaking well in the Gulf of Mexico. I was about to post to Facebook that this must be a sure sign that God was not happy with BP when, literally out of the blue, lightning struck a 62-foot-tall statue of Jesus outside Solid Rock Church in Monroe, Ohio.

And burned the graven image to the ground.

It didn't take long for a parishioner of Solid Rock to claim in early Associated Press versions of the story that the lightning strike must have indicated God's displeasure with the church.

This logic took me straight back to a story woven by my mother.

When I was growing up, each time an electrical storm rolled in Mom sat, huddled and trembling in fear, at the bottom of the steps that led to our home's second floor. Why? Because when she was a child, lightning had struck the chimney of her house. Her mother—the same sweet, arthritis-crippled grandma who always smiled and provided milk and cookies for me—told Mom and her sisters that God had caused lightning to strike the chimney because they were bad girls. This, I'm sure, was standard parenting technique in the 1920s, but it qualifies as child abuse.

A somewhat more rational and refreshing take on the Ohio strike came from Darlene Bishop, co-pastor of Solid Rock, who told media that she was relieved that lightning had struck the statue and not a home for at-risk women next door to the church.

"I told them, 'It looks like Jesus took a hit for you last night,'" she said.

Maybe.

I've never been one to reduce God to the image of Thor, hurling lightning bolts at people because he's angry or feeling mischievous. If this were so, the Philadelphia Flyers would have been struck by lightning multiple times in the last decade alone.

Thinking that God forces people into bankruptcy to prove a point about money management or causes them to drive cars into trees to punish them is the prime example of man trying to remake God in man's own image, of ascribing to God the petty interests on which we hang our hopes and dreams each day.

I see no hidden messages in the June 15 lightning strikes. The BP tanker just presented a great target for a random discharge of electricity from a storm cloud. As did the metal-framed statue of Jesus.

But if there was a hidden message in either, I vote for there being one in Ohio.

Something like, "Don't spend so much money on a Paul Bunyan-sized Jesus when you could use it to help those in need right across the street."

Observe the statue of limitations.

A Line Drawn in the Sand

Author's note: This column first appeared in 1990 during the Gulf War.

In the movie "Monty Python and the Holy Grail," a skewed retelling of the Arthurian legend, the king and his band of knights very errant, confronted by a killer rabbit, call upon the monk Brother Maynard to read from the "Book of Armaments." He does so, as follows:

And St. Attila raised the hand grenade up on high saying "O Lord, bless this thy hand grenade that with it thou mayest blow thine enemies to tiny bits, in thy mercy."

Then, after the Holy Hand Grenade of Antioch has reduced Mr. Bunny to rabbit pellets, the knights cry out: "Praise be the Lord!"

The scene—indeed, the entire movie—is a parody, of course. But it illustrated wonderfully an assumption that every warring people since the beginning of times surely has made: God is on our side. Men of every faith, even pagan, from the depths of their foxholes if not their souls, have at one time or another prayed for someone or something on high to help them smite their enemies.

129

Naturally, each assumes the higher power will acknowledge his prayer only.

Maybe that's why one member of Claysville United Presbyterian Church was outraged last week.

Shepherded by the husband-and-wife pastoral team of the Revs. Jan and Tim Devine, the members of Claysville United Presbyterian since January 16, the day the Gulf War began, have participated in weekly prayer services. Services are held not only to support American troops in the Persian Gulf but to encourage attendees to examine their own souls, seeking out answers to the riddle of how Christians should react in time of war. The Devines also publish a monthly congregational newsletter, which last week apparently caused one woman to run out of cheeks to turn.

That woman called the *Observer-Reporter*—anonymously—and told an editor that she and her husband, whom she said was a member of the church, were appalled by a letter the Devines had reprinted for their congregations. She mailed a copy of the newsletter to the O-R.

Written by the Rev. Jim Renfrew, pastor of Grace Presbyterian Church in Rochester, New York, and first published in a denominational magazine before the war began, the letter the caller branded offensive asked a poignant question that is best stated in the words of its author.

After noting the magazine's coverage of U.S. chaplains and troops in the Persian Gulf and thanking editors for printing an address for American troops serving there, Renfrew wrote:

What was lacking was some indication as to how we might address correspondence to ... the Iraqi forces. As Christians we acknowledge that the cross supersedes any boundary or flag. The members of my church have expressed strong support [for American troops in the Middle East], while ... expressing many serious doubts about the wisdom of the policy that led to this massive ... deployment. They are also very critical of the Iraqi government's invasion of Kuwait, but do not hold individual Iraqi soldiers responsible for their being in that country. Don't these Iraqi soldiers also deserve to hear from us? They, too, are far from their families, serving in harsh desert conditions, wondering if each day might be their-last. ... How about it?

Closing the reprint was the address of the Iraqi Embassy in Washington, D.C.

My phone call on Wednesday caught the Devines by surprise. They declined to respond to the woman's complaint, which I had summarized. The complainant had neither called nor approached her or her husband, Mrs. Devine said, nor had any others who might have been offended by Renfrew's letter.

"Our church's position has been one of support [for American troops]," her husband said. "We invite people to attend our weekly prayer services. We just offered the letter as food for thought."

And so the Devines became workers in God's cafeteria.

My guess is it's not the first time a morsel doled out there has refused to sit comfortably in the belly of the brain. Hard it is to practice what we preach, even harder to practice what has been preached to us.

I could not reach Renfrew; a church custodian told me he is away on study leave for several weeks. I'm sorry for that, not simply because the horse's mouth is always the best source, but because I wanted to thank him for obliterating what, for me, had been a line drawn in the sand. A line between coalition and Iraqi forces. A line between human beings.

Each day of the war I have wrestled with my feelings, cheering allied victories even while knowing that because of them, somewhere, an Iraqi weeps. Renfrew makes sense; by God, he makes sense. Aid and comfort to the enemy be damned.

In adopting a faith, we cannot choose tenets piecemeal, chucking out those inconvenient enough to cause discomfort. The pill of religion—whether dispensed in Christian, Islamic, Buddhist, Shintoist, Hindu, Jewish or any other form—is meant to be swallowed whole.

If the creed fits, live it.

No one promised it would be easy.

Season's Greetings From Nazareth

One tradition that seems to have passed with the advent of email is the family Christmas newsletter. At one time almost every family received a typewritten epistle from someone they hardly knew or hadn't seen in years. After desktop publishing became available, these even took on the appearance of a newspaper. I suppose people write Christmas blogs now.

In any case, the hallmark of these Christmas communiques is that they contain bits of mundane information about the daily workings of a family: Billy cut his first tooth; Joe lost his job; we have a new house; the cat died. Above all, Christmas newsletters prove that every family struggles with the day-to-day business of being human.

With this in mind, I present what I think the very first Christmas newsletter must have said.

*　　*　　*

Hello all!!!

Well, it's been almost a year since little Jesus was born, and what a year it has been! If I'd known what I was getting into, I'd have told that angel to take a hike. (ha ha) But seriously, we are happy to have the patter of little feet around the house, and we appreciate the joys of parenthood. But like I said, what a year!

It started out, of course, with our having to sleep in a stable over in Bethlehem—and all because my schmoe of a husband (Hey ... I kid!) forgot to reserve a room. Then there was the little matter of his misplacing his wallet and trying to pay with dried dates. But the innkeeper was kind, although I'm still picking straw out of my hair. (ha ha)

Then of course we had to flee to Egypt to avoid Herod's men, and me having packed only one outfit—and NOT one that looks good in the desert, if you know what I mean. What a trek! But we did get to see the Pyramids and the Sphinx (who looks like my mother-in-law!!!) Oh ... you should have seen the faces of the tour guides when Joseph told them that he thought those huge things had been built by aliens. What a schlemiel he is! But a good father.

Anyway, after the angel told Joseph the coast was clear back home, we schlepped our stuff back to Nazareth and settled in. A word of warning— make sure you get the neighbors to feed your fish while you're away, even if you have to leave in the middle of the night. What a mess!

Since we got back, Joseph has been busy in the shop and is a wizard with wood—great with his hands in general, although his little "experiment" with making diapers out of fig leaves was a disaster, let me tell you. Adam and Eve must've had a better tailor. (ha ha)

So it's really been a hectic year. But we're thankful that Joseph is working, even if the Roman Senate did extend tax breaks for the rich again.

That's about it. Now that the holidays are upon us, we want to share the joy of the season with you—even though that scamp Jesus has knocked over the menorah more than once! I can't wait till he's old enough for medical school!!! (ha ha)

Happy Holidays!!!! (Don't want to offend our non-Jewish friends!)

Mary, Joseph and Jesus

Social-isms

The columns in this section don't lend themselves to easy categorization. Let's just say that these are takes on our society in general—and the everlasting, remarkable and amazing plasticity that lets us ignore inconvenient inconsistencies, such as polluting resources with plastic bottles discarded after we drink bottled water to avoid ingesting pollutants.

* If you don't speak Spanish, there is a translation for you hidden somewhere in this section. Think of it as a placemat at Denny's.

Make Every Day Earth Day

Author's note: This column first appeared in 1990 on the eve of the celebration of the 20th Earth Day.

A simpler time it was in 1923, when poet Robert Frost proclaimed his preference for a fiery end to this world. Then, his lone proffered alternative was ice. How fortunate Frost was to have died before he faced the additional possibility of being buried under disposable diapers.

But enough throwaway humor. For the rest of this Monday-before-Earth Day column, let me wax mostly serious. You see, Frost was not far wrong—we may yet roast because chlorofluorocarbons have depleted the Earth's ozone layer; we may yet freeze because our fossil fuels have been exhausted. But, like Frost, surely we will die before either happens. Why should we care?

Because it is not our world in which we live. It is our children's.

This is not a virgin idea, by any means. Parents worth their salt always have lived not for themselves, but for their offspring, and long before the words "environmentally conscious" became for-

137

ever inseparable in print. I have known this for some time.

But in 1970, when the first Earth Day took place, I did not understand the motivation of parents. And one year ago, before I forgot the 19th anniversary of Earth Day, I was only beginning to appreciate it. Now I both understand and appreciate.

I write today as the father of a 13-month-old son, our first child. He has changed radically in the nearly 400 days since he arrived, but not so much as I. Friends told me this change would take place. I did not believe them.

Fear not, this column won't degenerate into the reverie of a man experiencing in his fourth decade the joys of fatherhood for the first time. No, this column will degenerate into something even harder to stomach: logic.

Indulge me here. Allow, first, a metaphor: Earth as mankind's bedroom. Next, an inductive leap: Considering the lousy jobs most of us did of cleaning our rooms as children, it should come as no surprise that, as adults, we stand in jeopardy of having our squatting rights to Bedroom Earth usurped by environmental dustballs born of our negligence.

And, finally, logic: Unlike our childhood rooms, Earth is not something we can move away from. This is the new, environmentally conscious me (NECM) writing now. You, there in the back! Pay attention!

Let me admit straight away that my transfiguration is incomplete. Our baby wears disposable diapers, although I know they clog our landfills and likely won't disappear until the sun has swollen and exploded and maybe not even then. But I'm told the washing of cloth diapers introduces into our water pollutants that might be harder on the environment than are plowed-under Pampers. In other words, all diapers stink—ecologically and olfactorily. So using disposables is the one compromise I allow the NECM. It wasn't always.

The borough we live in began a non-mandatory pilot recycling program six months ago. We did not participate until, in writing this column, I felt guilty about admitting we did not participate.

That changed, but still I am not perfect; becoming the NECM is hard work. So hard, in fact, that not long ago my onboard accountability avoidance system would have steered me right around the task. But there's something about being wakened each morning by a tiny replica of yourself that makes responsibility somehow more palatable. Joyful, even.

So help me clean our room.

Let's make it easy to start. This Sunday—Earth Day—try to begin to understand and appreciate our parents' desire to make a better world for their children. If you already understand, seek out someone who does not and reason with him. And if that doesn't work, give him a swift kick in the Huggies. Both accomplish the same end; both are equally justifiable.

For if we are to believe that Earth abides forever, we must not let another generation fade away.

My School Board President Rescued Me From Mariachi

Author's note: This column first appeared in 2013, after singer/teenage tart Miley Cyrus suggestively twerked during the Grammy Awards telecast.

Last week administrators from the Peters Township School District stopped a dance on school property because of what one board member characterized as "massive twerking" by attendees.

If you're a parent who eschews social media or any type of communication device other than a landline telephone, here's a definition of "twerking" provided by Wikipedia:

Twerking is a type of dancing in which an individual dances to popular music in a sexually provocative manner involving thrusting hip movements and a low squatting stance.

If your landline telephone still has a dial, Wikipedia is kind enough to also provide definitions for "thrusting hip movements" and a "low squatting stance."

141

If that's not enough, Google "Miley Cyrus."

School board members had varying responses when contacted by the media about what I like to call "Twerkapalooza." Perhaps the most unusual response came from William Merrell, who said he had contacted the local Arthur Murray dance studio to see what kinds of dance classes they offered. I assume his purpose was to ensure that students learn to twerk correctly.

I'm kidding, of course. Mr. Merrell no doubt wishes students to learn one of the "nice" dances taught at the Murray studios. The merengue, perhaps, which the studio describes as "considered too scandalous when it was introduced to the United States in 1941." Or swing dancing, of which in 1938 the *Ave Maria*, a newspaper published by the University of Notre Dame, said: "A degenerate and demoralized musical system is given a disgusting christening as 'swing' and turned loose to gnaw away the moral fiber of our young people."

The Charleston, perhaps? "Any lover of the beautiful will die rather than be associated with the Charleston," said the vicar of St. Aidan's, Bristol, England, in 1926. "It is neurotic! It is rotten! It stinks! Phew, open the windows."

Thank God that the president of my own school board was cut from the same cloth.

It was the night of our high school's 1965 Christmas semi-formal. Vic Maybray Sr.'s small dance combo provided the music. They were a safe choice, the school board figured, because leader Vic was in his mid-fifties and the band members wore matching plaid sportcoats. There would be none of the dreaded Beatles music that was sweeping our small town. But about 15 minutes into the band's first set, something went terribly wrong.

The bass drum thumped a steady four—bomp, bomp, bomp, bomp—followed by a low blat from the trombone that made it sound like Satan's Sackbut: BWAAAAAAWWWWW!!!!! Then his trumpet minions kicked in. Couples of every stripe—cheerleaders and jocks, nerds and nerdesses, hoodlums and molls—flooded the gymnasium floor and began to gyrate obscenely. The tune was the

Herb Alpert and the Tijuana Brass version of "A Taste of Honey."

Before "Honey" had dripped its last, the president of the school board made his way to the bandstand and talked agitatedly with Vic, who stood conducting with his left hand while shaking his head several times. Finally, Vic nodded—grudgingly, it seemed—and the president sauntered away. The rest of the band's set—and, indeed, everything else it played that night—was anchored firmly in the demilitarized zone between foxtrot and cha-cha. Vic, whose daughter had been my classmate since first grade, told me during the break that the head of the school board had instructed, "No more of this crap!"

For this I—and those who would graduate over the next four years—have him to thank for rescuing us from a debauched future powered by anglicized mariachi music.

No doubt the students of Peters Township High School will look back at 2013, raise their eyes to Heaven and intone, "There but for the grace of God twerk I."

Good lord! You actually turned the book upside down! My editor wanted me to disappoint you and not translate, but I just can't. "¡Lucha la potencia!"="Fight the power!" De nada, gringo.

Pushing the Envelope

Among the many difficult questions America faces in the 21st century, none is tougher than this: Do dogs still hate mailmen?

I know, I know—"mail carriers." But should any female mailman take offense at my supposed sexism and want to "deliver" something to me, well ... I have a pit bull.

I'll confess that this shocking question really hadn't occurred to me until a friend pointed out that her cats no longer come running to the kitchen at the sound of a can opener because their food now is packed in pop-top cans. In what other ways, she postulated, might animals have adapted in today's electronic world? For example, do squirrels stand just outside a yard, sticking their tongues out at dogs imprisoned by an "invisible fence?"

I know animals adapt. A dog I owned, no matter how soundly asleep, bolted to her feet the second I used the remote control to turn off the TV. She figured I was about to leave the room and didn't want to be left behind. If I didn't leave the room after turning off the TV, her eyes said, "Liar!" Perhaps this is why she ate the remote.

Like most people who work days, I seldom see a mailman—I mean sexless uniformed government courier. Mail is delivered by hand? Letters might just as well materialize in my box via some Star Trek-like atom-rearrangement-and-transmission scheme for all I know. So I couldn't assure my friend that dogs still hate mailmen, or if they merely sit at a computer and bite the mouse when email arrives.

But I live next to a guy who has two Rottweilers that he claims are ex-Navy SEALs. He says that shortly after 9/11, his dogs were outfitted with helmets and night-vision goggles, then dropped into Pakistan. They were dragging Osama Bin Laden across the border by the scruff of his neck when an Afghani mailman walked by and ...

That's pretty convincing proof that dogs still hate mailmen. But I thought it best to seek corroboration of my conclusion. That's why I stopped at the post office on my way to work on Tuesday. OK, I needed a stamp, too.

"I want to mail this first class," I said, handing my letter to the clerk

"One stamp?" she said, an eyebrow upraised.

Under pressure, I said, "Um ... 10 stamps?"

"Plus this one?"

"Yes."

"So ... you want 11 stamps, not 10!"

"You are sharp for this early in the morning," I said. She glowered.

Seeking to regain her favor, I said: "My friend wonders if, now that everyone uses email, dogs still hate mailmen," I blurted out.

Her eyes widened; both eyebrows rose.

"Oh my, yes!" she said. "They hate them and chase them and bite them. That behavior has been handed down by dogs for generations."

Now, that's intriguing. A USPS employee, who clearly has inside information, would have us believe that the long history of dog vs. mailman is not the product of evolution. Instead, it can be traced to Noah and the pair of mail carriers (one male, one female) he took aboard the Ark, along with the archetypal Lady and the Tramp. Then something went terribly wrong. Perhaps the first mailman threw a bone overboard and told Lady to fetch.

So, since the fateful day the Ark struck Ararat, cur and courier have been mortal enemies. Canine whelps have learned at their grandsires' haunches that mailmen are not to be trusted.

Call it "Intellidog Design."

Mayberry R.I.P.

I have to believe it's no coincidence that on the same day Public Radio International (PRI) aired a segment called "Are we afraid of free time?" I also heard that Andy Griffith had died.

Griffith was best known as the star of "The Andy Griffith Show," the gentle 1960s comedy in which he played Sheriff Andy Taylor of the fictional town of Mayberry, North Carolina. The show has been perpetually in reruns since 1968, so most Americans between the ages of 9 and 90 have been exposed to the its homespun philosophy. Which could be summed up as a variation of a quote attributed to such diverse sources as poet Ralph Waldo Emerson and Capt. Jack Sparrow: "It's not the destination, it's the journey."

What a wonderful philosophy it is.

The PRI segment was prompted by "The Busy Trap," a *New York Times Opinionator* article by Tim Kreider, who notes that many of his friends claim to be busy—too busy—these days. But not because they have to be. "They're busy because of their own ambition or drive or anxiety," Kreider observes, "because they're addicted to busyness and dread what they might have to face in its absence."

Watching people talking on cellphones while driving, texting at ballgames and concerts or taking a supposedly quiet walk in the woods with iPods blaring, I have to agree. We're the wired wireless generation.

The citizens of Mayberry were never too busy. Sure, there were dances and Ladies Aid Society meetings and canning festivals to attend, but Mayberryites always managed to find time not only for those, but also to hang around Floyd's barber shop or sit on the front porch in the evenings, fanning themselves while someone played the guitar. Life was idyllic.

The mayor never had to cut funding for mass transit because there was none—unless eight neighbors carpooling to the church social qualifies. Unemployment seemed to be limited to Otis, the lovable town drunk, or the odd hobo who passed through, teaching Opie a valuable lesson in the process. Healthcare wasn't an issue because if you couldn't pay the doctor, he'd carry you for a few months.

And there was room for the odd duck in Mayberry. The definition of "acceptable" was pretty broad. Today, Barney would be diagnosed with social-anxiety-panic-attack-delusions-of-grandeur disorder and medicated into conduct more becoming a law enforcement officer. Opie would be on Ritalin, and Aunt Bee would be undergoing weekly 45-minute sessions with a psychiatrist to cure her of her compulsive need to shove baked goods at passers-by.

Mayberry residents just took Barney, Opie and Aunt Bee for what they were—good folks with quirks, whose value to the community far outweighed the little inconveniences that their oddities imposed on their neighbors. I have the feeling that even if Goober and Howard had expressed the desire to marry each other, people still would have welcomed them at the church social. That sort of fond acceptance seems linked to being less busy with one's self-important concerns and more busy helping others to feel valued. Perhaps they were country bumpkins, but by the end of each episode, it was clear that being a bumpkin might not be so bad.

Maybe it's time for each of us to get in touch with our inner bumpkin. Disconnect from the world now and then. Hit the walking trail without your cellphone and iPod. Leave your Droid in the car when you go into a restaurant. Figure out what you like about your co-workers instead of what drives you crazy. Hide the video games. Don't tweet. Make your Facebook status "In Mayberry."

Whether you believe in an afterlife, reincarnation or simply that nothing at all lies beyond, the simple fact is that each of us has the power to create Heaven or Hell—for ourselves and for others—right here on Earth.

Baby, baby, it's a wired world.

But in my mind, I'm goin' to Carolina.

Mulch Ado About Nothing

Author's note: This column was one of three for which I won the Keystone Press Award in 1992.

They were leaning there against the wall of the convenience store on a cold Wednesday afternoon, waiting for someone to pick them up and give them a ride home: three lonely young Christmas trees.

But Bill Sukolsky, who manages CoGo's at the corner of Pike and Cherry streets in Houston[1], said the trio wouldn't have long to wait.

"They're what's left of my first shipment," Sukolsky said. "We'll have more by the end of the week. They've been moving real well."

With good reason. At $20 for any tree, CoGo's conifers are priced right. The same at East Pike and Euclid in Canonsburg[2], where CoGo's corner market has the market cornered. Business is good.

But I feel bad. Neither Canonsburg nor Houston has fulfilled the Christmas-tree-lot quota for towns their sizes. At least, not in the way I remember from my youth.

Back then, formerly vacant lots—seemingly one in every block—became pine forests overnight each December 1. I knew by first name half the old men who pounded their mittened hands together, waiting while I rejected tree after tree for slight curvature of the pine until I found the perfect specimen. It was traditional.

But now, only a single, old-fashioned, formerly vacant lot at the corner of Washington and East McMurray roads in Peters Township stands out from the concrete blur between Pittsburgh and Washington. It's as I remember these lots: crammed with trees; clear, 60-watt bulbs strung between two-by-fours; a handmade tree-measuring pole, red painted numerals ticking off feet in 1-foot increments up to 10. Drive by. See if, for one magical instant, your childhood doesn't return.

At least until the traffic signal changes.

Then drive down Route 519 in North Strabane[3], where Tom Whalen sells cut "live" trees at his nursery. For $19.95, you'll get a 6-foot Scotch pine. For $40 more, Tom will let you adopt a living tree, complete with root ball for post-Yule planting.

But don't be cheap, Whalen warned. If the root ball is skimpy, the tree will be wimpy, he explained. The tree might die when planted. So do it right. But with right costing $59.95, Tom said, cut trees outsell living trees 1,000-to-1.

There are other options. For roughly $25, you can still stalk and cut the elusive evergreen at Hozak's Christmas Tree Farm in Clinton. And artificial trees, of course, grow anywhere. Happily, a salesman at Pool City told me Americans long ago rejected silver aluminum trees like the one my brother Harry foisted on my family in 1960. "It'll save us money in the long run," Harry said.

In a warm holiday scene my family will forever cherish, we trashed the tin tree—limb by chromium limb—six years later, after Harry was married and could no longer protect his investment.

But for sheer Yuletide innovation, you've got to hand it to the Saab-sauna connection—those nutty Swedes—who this year gifted us with Rent-A-Tree.

IKEA, the Swedish-owned furniture store newly opened in Robinson Town Center on the Parkway West, made a limited number of rental—yes, rental—trees available Thursday.

Here was the deal, according to IKEA spokeswomen Chrissie: For 20 bucks, you could pick out one cut, live Douglas fir, up to 8 feet tall.

Return the tree to be mulched on either Jan. 6 or 13 and leave with a $10 rebate and, if you wish, the mulch, the Swedish word for which is pronounced, "Yous-tu-be-uh-tree."

Rent a tree? I don't know. Poet Joyce Kilmer was right: Only God can make a tree.

But maybe he should've retained the marketing rights.

[1-3] *Houston, Canonsburg and North Strabane Township—small communities near Washington, Pa.—were all part of my "beat" when I first joined the* Observer-Reporter.

Remembering Occupy Plymouth

Author's note: This column first appeared in 2011, just after the Occupy Wall Street movement made headlines. How, I wondered, might the Pilgrim Fathers have dealt with such protests?

It was the day after Thanksgiving 1622, and William Bradford, governor of Plymouth Colony, was not a happy man.

Only a couple days prior, the 10-member Behemoth Committee had failed to reach agreement on a plan to lower the colony's debt, which somehow had skyrocketed in just over a year to nearly £22,000. The fools! It had taken only about an hour for the Occupy Plymouth protesters to show up outside his front door. Followed by the town criers.

And just the week before the coach of the New Plymouth Middle School stoolball[1] team had been caught showering with two of the boys. Firing the athletic director hadn't helped. "Maintaineth thy demeanor," Mrs. Bradford had counseled. But it hadn't been easy—especially after Capt. Miles Standish, head of the Plymouth militia, had ordered his security force to spray the Occupy protestors with skunk juice. A craftsman had managed to get the whole thing down on parchment using a piece of charred wood from a burning wagon. The parchment had gone viral.

Bradford was exhausted. He had dragged himself to bed near midnight on what everyone was calling "Thanksgiving II" but had been unable to sleep. How could things have become so arsy-varsy[2] in only one year?

Bradford recalled the feast of 1621 as a day of great celebration. The colony's harvest had been better than they'd hoped, so they'd invited Squanto, Samoset and Massasoit, the local Indian leaders, over for the Detroit Lions game. They'd brought with them about 90 of their kin and a good sampling of baked maize snacks—but had forgotten the dip. Still, even though the colonists had run out of beer by halftime, no one had complained. These Indians weren't a bad bunch, Bradford had thought. So it was with anticipation that he had invited them back a year hence. What a mistake!

The Indians had arrived late, claiming that they'd been detained at a wild party at "the other colony." Only after Standish and his men had stumbled through the woods for hours in search of more Englishmen had Squanto admitted that they'd been joking. Standish had been unable to see the humor. "Squanto?" Standish had said, poking the Indian in the chest. "Verily ... it doest sound like a maiden's name to my ears!"

Next, although the Indians had brought maize chips *and* dip this year, some of the colonists had complained that something didn't taste quite right. Standish—while using the tip of his pike as a toothpick—had suggested that the appetizer might contain bits of the dog missing from the colony for the last few days. Massasoit had denied it vehemently. But he had been wearing the dog's collar.

Then there was the matter of the handmade centerpiece that John and Priscilla Alden had presented to Mrs. Massasoit. Still a bit miffed after losing Priscilla's affections to Alden, Standish had "accidentally" knocked the centerpiece off the table, at which point the gift had split—revealing it to be Plymouth Rock, painted red. A fight had been avoided only because Samoset had whipped out a ukulele and led everyone in a rollicking tune involving two French sailors and a large sea bass. And besides—even the Indians had to admit that Priscilla's paint job was first class.

Things finally had been looking up when, around 11 o'clock, Mrs. Bradford had lost her cool, grabbed two of Massasoit's 11 kids by the scruffs of their necks, and screamed, "Stop acting like a bunch of wild Indians!"

Massasoit and the others had departed in a huff. "Stuff turkey!" Bradford thought he had heard one of them say over his shoulder. No wonder he'd been unable to sleep.

He slouched, shook his head and sighed. Thanksgiving III probably wasn't going to happen.

But if it did, Standish had plenty of skunk juice left.

[1]*Stoolball: A form of cricket that was popular at the time of Plymouth's founding.*

[2]*Arsy-varsy: 17th century variation of "ass-backwards."*

Shoring Up the High Ground

I've been able to weather the ebb and flow of life by holding on to the inflated belief that within any situation, humor can be found. It's a dual-edged sword because people come to expect me to be constantly "on." But I'm not always funny. Sometimes I'm just having a bad flair day. And sometimes humor can be hard to find.

There's been a lot of talk about civility—or, rather, the lack thereof—in political discourse following the Jan. 8, 2011, shooting of Arizona Rep. Gabrielle Giffords. I'm not entirely sure that inflammatory political speech led directly to the rampage. But there's no doubt in my mind that civility—and not just in political exchanges—has been on its deathbed in America for roughly 30 years.

Examples abound in everyday life. Who among us has not been flipped off by a driver? Who hasn't had his view at a concert obscured by people standing up in the rows ahead—people who become belligerent and vulgar when asked to sit down? Who hasn't had his pleasant country outing ruined by the cranked boombox of the picnickers in an adjacent shelter? Who hasn't, while trapped in an elevator, become involuntarily privy to the rantings of a cellphone user? Who hasn't had his opinion shouted down or dismissed out of hand because it didn't coincide with another's?

I used to think that as long as even one person chose to take the high ground, civility would continue on life support, even if its relatives—decorum, decency, discretion and common sense—were arguing over whether to pull the plug. Now I'm not so sure. More and more, people armed with verbal picks and shovels are undermining the high ground in what seems to be an attempt to bring it down to gutter level. They do it in many ways.

There's the classic "non-apology apology": "I'm sorry that you were offended by what I said." Not, "I'm sorry that I spoke too quickly, that I didn't consider that my choice of words might be offensive to you." Rather, "I'm sorry you were offended" neatly transfers the guilt to the listener, implying that said listener made the mistake of taking offense.

There's "My remarks were taken out of context," which has much in common with another defense: "That's not what I intended." Like the non-apology apology, these attempts to spin the meaning of an ambiguous statement also have the benefit of turning the offended party into the offender—as in, "I'm offended that you, being stupid, couldn't understand what I really meant to say."

"That's not what I intended" came into play when a member of former vice-presidential candidate Sarah Palin's staff attempted to convince skeptics that the "crosshairs" placed on a political map that included Rep. Giffords' district were actually "surveyor's sights." I'm willing to wager that if you had taken a poll of Americans prior to the Arizona shootings, most could not have identified a surveyor's transit, let alone have known that it uses a sighting mechanism similar to those used on rifles. Splitting crosshairs, I call it. Rather like painting a swastika on the side of your house and claiming it was meant to evoke only its Hindu usage.

In fairness, I must point out that Democrats also have used crosshairs on maps to indicate districts where politicians might be "vulnerable," and that politics has been rife with bellicose verbiage, from all parties, for centuries: "targeted districts"; "battle-ground states"; "Don't retreat! Reload!" Still, I believe that the lack of civility in politics is but a reflection of an ingrained belief that as Americans, we are endowed by our creator with the inalienable right to speak without thinking.

How wrong we are.

Poet John Donne had it right when he said: "No man is an island entire of itself; every man is a piece of the continent, a part of the main. ..."

His point was the death of any one man affects all of us because we are part of the whole of mankind. At least that's the Cliffs Notes interpretation.

So, too, would the death of civility affect all of us. I say this not in jest, although I know that is what is expected of me.

Uneasy lies the head that wears the lampshade.

Square Peg, Round Ball

Author's note: This column first appeared in 2013.

When I was in elementary school and having trouble with my multiplication tables, my father used a simple motivational technique: He smacked me in the back of the head with his hand. When I started to cry, he offered these tender words: "Sissy! We'll put pink ribbons in your hair!" Then he smacked me again.

I thought of Dad last week when I heard about the dismissal of Rutgers University basketball coach Mike Rice. Rutgers president Robert Barchi fired Rice April 3 after viewing a video, compiled over a period of a year from recording of practices, in which Rice was seen both physically and verbally abusing players and using homophobic slurs to describe their play.

Rutgers officials had been made aware of the videos in November but, rather than fire Rice, chose to suspend him for three games and fine him $50,000. The dismissal came only after the videos were made public by *Outside the Lines*.

Public reaction after the announcement of Rice's firing was swift and predictable. Some denounced Rutgers officials for having taken so long to act. Others condemned Rice for having "crossed the line."

On local sports talk radio, former players came forth to say that such treatment is commonplace in sports. A few defended Rice. Sports is tough, they said. Being bullied, pushed, kicked, hit with a ball and being called "faggot" is all part of a strategy that produces better players.

Really? If this be true, why not chain players to a post and whip them? It supposedly did wonders for productivity at Southern plantations.

More troubling than the defense of Rice by former players is the logic rolled out by those who said such coaching tactics are commonplace. Ah! The old "everybody does it" defense. Remember how well that defense worked when your mom countered with, "And if everybody jumped off the bridge, would you?" It's still indefensible. Ubiquitousness does not justify an odious practice.

Even more puzzling was the veiled suggestion by one talk show host that the incriminating video was leaked by former Rutgers assistant coach Eric Murdock. Fired by the university after he blew the whistle on Rice, Murdock had a good reason to leak the video, the host said. But that doesn't excuse Rice's actions.

The same host also said that Murdock had compiled the video from many recorded practices. "Put all together, it looks worse than it is," he said.

Absolutely! And the Nazis killed 6 million Jews over six years, but it looks much worse when compressed into a 1-hour PBS special.

Exactly why, in 2013, is it still commonplace to "motivate" athletes, employees or elementary school children by calling them sissies, queers and faggots? Oh, I know: If we can't stop "them" from destroying the family unit, at least we can prevent "their kind" from tainting the purity of collegiate and professional sports.

It's time for me to admit something. I come before you today a master of multiplication—thanks largely to the invention of the pocket calculator. My dad's motivational techniques did nothing to improve my math, just as his forcing me to wear a crewcut until I was 17 did nothing to stop me from growing my hair long as soon as I was 18. Just as his insistence that I would never make a living as a musician did nothing to deter me.

In fact, Dad's use of physical and verbal abuse as a parenting tool did only one thing: it made him a jerk.

Just like Mike Rice.

When Words Collide

A s a writer, I have a love affair with words. I embrace 'em all—long or short, mono- or poly-syllabic. And even blue words. So I'm a bit puzzled as to why editors waited almost 25 years before deciding that "F-bomb" is worthy of inclusion, along with 100 other "new" words, in the latest edition of the Merriam-Webster Collegiate Dictionary. That's a long freakin' time. Maybe they had an "aha moment." That's one of the other "new" words they added.

A member of the dictionary's editing team tells the Associated Press that she and her colleagues traced the first published occurrence of F-bomb back to 1988, in a *Newsday* story in which the late baseball player Gary Carter said that he had given up using profanity.

Who knows how many times since Carter's divulgence the term has been used? A bunch, I'm guessing. But now it's officially in the dictionary.

Thanks, Merriam-Webster! No longer will Americans think that F-bomb is one of the weapons the United States developed between the A-bomb and the H-bomb.

Online commenters—apparently unaware that the word for which F-bomb is a euphemism has been in dictionaries for many years—called it "a sad day for mankind" and "a grave mistake." So are war, poverty, genocide, starvation and mass murder. But they're in the dictionary, and no one seems annoyed.

F-bomb doesn't bother me. I'm more annoyed by some of the other words or phrases the Merriam-Webster crew added—ones I wish I never had to hear again. Like the aforementioned "aha moment," first used in 1939, "gamechanger" (1993), "shovel-ready" (1998) and "man cave" (1992). I suppose that "aha moment" is preferable to "epiphany," but only because if you tell your friends you had an epiphany, they will think the Three Wise Men came to visit your newborn son. And I suppose a "man cave" was "shovel ready" before being built.

Another term I can do without is "sea change," already in the Merriam-Webster and used by talking heads seemingly every time a major change occurs in anything except the level of an ocean. Likewise "untracked," which sports analysts constantly use to mean "getting on track." Listen: An "untracked" train lies on the ground like an "unbowled" guppie. Is that what you want your favorite team to do this season?

Newsmen, please stop saying politicians "doubled down" on asinine statements. How about substituting "repeated his idiotic comment"?

And then we have "to spite," constantly used by TV and radio reporters when what they really mean is "despite." "Iran presses ahead with its nuclear program to spite sanctions," one headline read.

Folks, you cut off your nose *to spite* your face. You go drinking with your buddies *despite* knowing that your fiancée will not like it. The next day, she stops sleeping with to you *to spite* you.

Yeah, I know ... there are more distressing things in life to be upset over, but I can't help it. Hackneyed phrases gall me.

I guess I've just got my panties in a wad.

The General, Pee Wee and Spidey

Author's note: This column first appeared in 2010.

We know that old soldiers just fade away. Apparently middle-aged soldiers dig their own graves.

Until last week, I had a mental picture of our military being led by gruff-talking, bullet-spitting, hard-drinking men patterned after John Wayne's Sgt. Stryker in "Sands of Iwo Jima." And by hard-drinking, I mean that they gulp down cocktails made with three parts jet fuel and one part napalm. Shaken, not stirred, dammit! And no stinking olive!

That image shattered when I heard that Gen. Stanley McChrystal, former commander of U.S. and NATO forces in Afghanistan, favors Bud Light Lime—a sissified beer if ever there was one.

Maybe you missed that information, although it was placed fairly high in a *Rolling Stone* profile of McChrystal that hit the newsstands last week. I did. Maybe you missed it because you were depressed by the ouster of the U.S. soccer team from the World Cup matches by Ghana—a sissified nation if ever there was one.

But I'm betting you missed the Bud Light Lime reference because you, too, were saying "Whaaaaaaaaa?" after learning that in the article, McChrystal and his staff had said less-than-flattering things about Vice-President Joe Biden. And about many of the civilians charged with overseeing U.S. policy in Afghanistan. And, although it didn't make the article, probably about Bo, President Obama's Portuguese Water Dog—a sissified mutt if ever there was one.

Of course Obama removed McChrystal from command forthwith; we all knew that would happen. America has multiple examples of a president removing an uppity commander: Lincoln vs. Gen. George McClelland; FDR vs. Gen. George Patton; Harry S. Truman vs. Gen. Douglas MacArthur.

I support Obama's decision. Not because McChrystal drinks a sissified beer. Not because at one point in the article the general pretended he didn't know who Biden is. And not even because he couldn't keep his staff from behaving like the frat boys in "Animal House" during the interview.

No, I support the removal of McChrystal because he, the man supposedly wise enough to run the Afghan counterinsurgency campaign, didn't have the common sense to go into a room with a reporter and keep his trap shut.

McChrystal and his defenders were quick to say that Michael Hastings, who conducted multiple interviews with McChrystal for *Rolling Stone*, broke the rules by publishing some quotes that the general and his staff thought were off the record.

Whaaaaaaaaa?

Look—I'm a former reporter, and even I wouldn't trust a journalist who was toting a tape recorder or a notebook without first getting in writing what was to be off the record and what was for publication. I wouldn't do interviews with my drunken buddies mouthing off and dancing in the background. I damn sure wouldn't admit that I drank Bud Light Lime. But most of all, I wouldn't say what was really on my mind if I thought for a second that it might cost me my job.

Hastings, of course, says he played by the rules. But I've seen enough Spider-Man movies to know that journalists don't always tell the truth. And—also as a former reporter—I know that many was the time when a source revealed in an interview the location of a closeted skeleton, then called an hour later to request that everything be off the record. I guess we'll never know for sure what happened in McChrystal's case.

But part of me thinks that maybe he pulled a Pee Wee.

Paul Reubens, who created the Pee Wee Herman character that was so popular almost three decades ago, was arrested in 1991, at the height of his fame, for indecent exposure in a Florida adult theater. Although he never admitted it, many think that Reubens purposely staged the incident to rid himself of the Pee Wee persona. So, maybe, did the general.

Those Spider-Man movies taught me one more thing: With great power comes great responsibility.

And you can quote me on that.

Vampires Suck It Up

Author's note: This column first appeared in 1993.

I'm wondering why the vampires have been silent. I'm wondering why the secret succubus society hasn't decided to bare its collective fangs over the release of "Bram Stoker's Dracula" on home video.

Maybe because the film is a love story. OK, so heads get lopped off, blood gets slurped and sucked and spilled and other verbs that begin with "S," but in the end, "Dracula" is really the story of a man so obsessed with a woman that he crosses oceans of time to be with her.

Kinda the same way we felt about the head cheerleader in high school, isn't it, guys?

But you'll have to admit that vampires have a right to hiss—or howl, or flap around, or turn into a vapor, depending on how the mood strikes them—over the public penchant for portraying them as the only bloodsucking geeks in existence, when all the time we know there are plenty of them in Congress.

Yet they remain strangely silent, while witches are so vocal.

Haven't you heard? Then let me quote an Associated Press story from 1992:

"Incensed over their persistent negative portrayal, a group of seven self-proclaimed witches denounced (Walt Disney's) 'Hocus Pocus' as another 'silly witch movie' that feeds into stereotypes without offering any redeeming images.

"'Witches do not murder people,' said Ruth Rhiannon, a Covenant of the Goddess minister and co-founder of the Circle of Aradia in Los Angeles. Rhiannon said she saw the movie over the weekend and demanded her money back.

"It's injurious to children who are learning, according to this film, that witches want to kill them," she said.

This is the second time in the last year that witches have set their cauldrons bubbling over their public image. Not long ago, witches in the U.S. armed forces complained that they are being persecuted by comrades in arms who do not want to count theirs a true religion. Now this.

I have met one witch, in 1970. She claimed to be a white witch and offered to keep me out of the army by taking a lock of my hair and casting a spell on the day of my draft physical.

"It's got nothing to do with the devil," she said. "Your soul is in no danger." I was 21. I let her have a hunk of my hair. And I was not drafted.

Whether this makes me a draft dodger or in league with Satan is not an issue that keeps me awake at night. But it's made me, if anything, ambivalent toward witches.

I don't want to offend anyone. If people claim to be witches, I'm not above burning them at the stake just to make them feel vindicated. If there's some doubt, I'll use the Bill Clinton method: I'll burn them, but I won't inhale.

You want to be a witch? Fine. But stop whining about being mistreated. Quitcher witchy bitchin'!

If I've met a vampire, I'm not aware of it. So, where are the vampires? Could it be that they don't exist? Or maybe they think they have been portrayed accurately on film through the ages.

If they're angry, maybe they're just sucking it up. They like a nice, low profile. But if the vampires of the world want to protest, count me in their camp.

There's an issue I can really sink my teeth into.

Driven to Tears

If I might be permitted to paraphrase a great old saying: If God had meant us to drive, he would have given us wheels.

Well, obviously, he did mean us to drive, because he did give us wheels. Unfortunately we attached them to cars.

Now, I have not always mistrusted automobiles. In fact, I loved the first vehicle I purchased—a 1951 Cadillac hearse I resurrected from a vacant lot in 1967 for $15. It was a great ride, let me tell you: 15,000 original miles; three-speed stick; straight-8; heavy-duty suspension; all leather interior; "electric sanders" mounted in each rear wheel well that, if ever my one-hearse sleigh became stuck in the snow, could at the flip of a dashboard-mounted switch, spew sand in front of each tire. A clever device, I thought, to prevent people from arriving late for their own funerals.

All this, however, didn't convince me to buy this bier wagon. What really sold me on it—aside from its being just morbid enough to offend adults—was that its previous owner was a venetian-blind repairman. Stenciled above the windshield in 8-inch-high white block letters was "THIS DRIVER IS A BLIND MAN." This prompted some unintended results.

An example: Parked across the street from our high school one day, awaiting my girlfriend, I heard a knock on the driver's side window. I rolled it down, at which point the knocker said, "You may find this amusing, but I do not."

He was an undertaker. It was only then that I realized I was parked in front of a funeral home. Maybe the "Blind Man" thing was true.

But such whims gave way to practicality. I no longer believe that people should buy automobiles to annoy adults. I now believe that cars are beings from Hell bent on the destruction of their owners. And I have proof.

My second car, a 1959 Ford, had the annoying habit of stalling in the middle of cross-traffic turns. My 1968 Volkswagen Beetle, purchased in 1970, thrice ran out of gasoline, once in the Fort Pitt Tunnels. My 1975 Volkswagen Rabbit managed to void itself of oil—at 70 mph in the middle of an Ohio freeway.

In 1980, my 1977 Honda Accord was converted into a Honda Accordion by a carload of beer-swilling foreign students who, after they had rear-ended me at a red light, tumbled out of their slightly dented car, slurred out something like, "Your car OK, buddy," and drove away.

You might think that I'd be due for a break after 16 years of bad luck. But in 1986, I bought the devil in-car-nate.

He was masquerading as a cute little red Renault Alliance. For two years, the Renault was a great car, mainly, I suspect, because during that time it lurked in my garage as I rode buses to work. Finally, when I changed jobs and began to drive it daily, the cute little red Renault revealed its true colors.

On my way home one evening, it channeled my '59 Ford and stalled in mid-turn, then refused to restart. This happened in one of Pittsburgh's least desirable sections—one so bad that police once bused in drug pushers to clean it up.

I walked to a pay phone where I was, for the first and probably last time in my life, approached by a Woman of Questionable Virtue. At least that's what most people would call a woman wearing satin hot pants, knee-high vinyl boots and a fur coat over a tank top in summer.

"Do you ... *need* something?" she asked.

"What I *need*," I growled, fumbling for a quarter, "is a new car."

The last I saw of her was the gleam of her fishnet nylons shimmering in the dusk as she retreated.

I had the demonic Renault towed to the satanic Renault garage where, two days later, a Mephistophelian Trained Renault Mechanic told me, "It starts now."

"What did you do?" I asked.

"We let it sit in the sun for a couple of hours and jiggled some wires."

Which wires?

"Black ones."

I traded the car for a Honda the next day. But before I drove the Honda off the lot, I took it aside, showed it pictures of its wife and children, and made a veiled threat to cut off its magneto if ever it failed me.

I know it was cruel.

Call me a car berater.

Thumbs Down to Texting

I email my columns to this newspaper. This proves that although I'm about to rant about technology, I'm no technophobe. I can't afford to be afraid of technology because I don't type very well.

I use the middle finger on each hand to enter letters, my left thumb for the space bar and my left pinky for the shift key. I'm not saying this is the best system, but it has worked since I was 9 years old, when I appropriated my sister's Smith-Corona typewriter. Spell-checking software saves me. But although my system of text entry may be broken, I see no need to fix it. Why should I when roughly half the population of the United States is typing using two thumbs?

I speak, of course, of texting. You know, the practice of using a perfectly serviceable voice-transmission device to send a message that takes 10 times longer to deliver than if you'd simply hit speed dial and—God forbid—spoken to your party.

Am I the only one who sees the idiocy of using a sophisticated device to less than its full capability? It's like Capt. James T. Kirk, surrounded by Klingons, flipping open his Communicator and typing, "BM ME ^ SKA T!"

"NT LGIKL!" Spock texts in reply.

I've seen people texting while driving, tempting me to text the offending driver's license number to the state police. A friend tells he watched a woman engrossed in texting walk into the back of his FedEx truck ... which was parked. The same friend, who I've known for 16 years, has never called me on my cellphone. He texts. Before I can answer his text, he texts several follow-up questions. I call to ask how he can type so bloody fast using his thumbs. He doesn't answer.

And am I the only one who doesn't understand why people would rather text than talk? Or why they can't stop texting at events that should demand their undivided attention?

For example, people were texting during the height of the Paul McCartney concert August 19. $250 a ticket, and their eyes weren't on one of the two surviving Beatles. I understand that the music was too loud for anyone to talk on a cellphone, but what could they possibly have been texting?

"NA NA NA, NA NA NA NA, NA NA NA NA, HEY JUDE!!!"?

But, really, Americans did just fine for roughly 220 years without its citizens having the ability to send text messages. What would the country be like if texting had been available to the founding fathers? Would Thomas Jefferson, in seclusion at Monticello, ever have finished the Declaration of Independence if he'd have been peppered with text messages from the somewhat prickly John Adams?

Adams: U R 2 SLO! WUT HV U GT?

Jefferson: WE D P PL O D USA ...

Adams: ROTFLMAO

You say I'm overreacting, that sometimes people text because they're somewhere where they can't talk. I can understand that. Maybe they're in church, where I've seen people whip out a smartphone as soon as the sermon begins. Which begs the question—WWJT: What Would Jesus Text?

"BLSD B D PEESMKRS ..."?

Doesn't work for me—and probably wouldn't have worked for

the people at the bottom of the Mount of Olives, where cellphones would have had fewer bars.

Look, folks: If you have something to share that's worth dragging out a cellphone, say it.

Texting is simply thumbing your prose at people.

It's the Same Old Song

Author's note: This column is one of three for which I won the Keystone Press Award in 1994.

So my friend comes in with an armload of vinyl record albums—dramatic interpretations of stories starring superheroes (Superman, Batman, The Flash) and hands them to my 4-year-old son, Steve.

"Thank you!" says Steve, excited to be given anything. "What are they?"

And it dawns on me that Steve—who has his own portable cassette recorder and can program our VCR and change the shiny little discs in our CD player—has never seen a long-playing phonograph record.

It's a record, I tell him. When I was your age, I explain, one of my greatest pleasures was to open the lid of my single-play Webcor record player, slap my yellow Davy Crockett 78 on the felt-covered turntable and listen to how the ol' coonskinner "kilt him a bar when he was only 3."

I don't bother to include that, because I didn't know then that "bar" is hillbilly talk for "bear," I thought for several years that Davy had been "killed in a bar when he was only 3." (They start 'em young in Kaintuck, I reckoned.)

Steve ignores me.

So I tell him a coal-black 78 rpm record called "Yosemite Sam" shattered into a million pieces when I slammed down the Webcor's lid with the oversized platter still on the turntable.

Still, Steve ignores me. He knows I'm lying because the coal-black discs he's now winging against the wall aren't even coming close to shattering.

I give up and lapse into melancholia. At last, I have become ancient. But when? I don't know. You tell me.

Was it when I stopped going out to bars because the cigarette smoke made my eyes water? Was it when all *Playboy* playmates began to look alike?

Or did it happen just a few weeks ago, when I failed to recognized the name of a single artist on Billboard's Top 20? Yeah. That must've been it.

How ironic. I once was a musician.* I don't mean the kind who plays in the high school band, then hangs it up after graduation. No, I made my living as a musician, playing bass in rock bands in western Pennsylvania and eastern Ohio for almost 20 years. When at 33 I found myself playing the same hellhole bars I'd played at 16, I quit.

These days I can't tell Sister Souljah from Sister Marietta, the nun who runs Steve's daycare center. Mind you, I've never heard Sister Marietta sing. I don't think I've ever heard Sister Souljah rap. But if I do, I'm sure she'll sound exactly like Sister Marietta.

When did I lose my ear? Probably when I became a father. No father can tolerate his offspring's choice of music. When I was 16, Dad swore that the Beatles and the Lovin' Spoonful and Sonny and Cher sounded exactly alike. Probably, Grandpa Molter told Dad that Glenn Miller and Tommy Dorsey and Benny Goodman all sounded the same, too—and not nearly as good as John Philip Sousa. It's just the natural progression of things.

Having been a musician, I'll never yell at Steve if, in 10 years, he lets his hair grow past his collar or dresses like his favorite rock star. Because I did that, too. But I don't know if I'll be able to stop myself from saying, "All that stuff you listen to sounds the same!" Because I say it now.

Barney the purple dinosaur's theme song—"I love you, you love me"? Sounds just like "This Old Man" to me.

It's the same old song, just like the Four Tops said. Or was it the Temptations?

I can't tell them apart anymore.

* *After staying out of the music business for almost 20 years, I started playing again in 2000 and now play bass regularly in several Pittsburgh bands.*

A Child's Garden of Curses

*Author's note: Some things can't be printed in a "family newspaper."
So this column never ran. But, sick to death of America's growing xe-
nophobia and tendency to force people into pigeonholes—especially by
certain political candidates—in late 2016 I began to compile a list of stereotypes that haven't received the attention they deserve. Here they are.
Why should Mexicans and Muslims take all the heat?*

The Irish: Drunken puh-tay-tuh eaters and papists. Have huge
families. Men wear suspenders and hobnail boots. Women wear
aprons, even in bed. Have red hair and millions of freckles. Lazy.

The Jews: Have huge hooked noses and kinky hair. Eat bagels.
Worship money. Killed Jesus. Lazy.

The Brits: Have bad teeth. Sticks up their asses. Country ruled
by a woman. Drive on wrong side of road. Call soccer "football."
Lazy.

American Indians: Vocabulary limited to "Ugh!" and "How!"
Love firewater. Killed Custer. Live in teepees. Wear headdresses.
Lazy.

Indian Indians: Ride elephants. Worship elephants. Smell like elephants. Talk in squeaky voices, almost like elephants. Lazy.

The Italians: Invented organized crime, pizza and spaghetti. Have huge families. Smell like garlic. Men wear pinstripe suits and fedoras and have mustaches. Women have mustaches. Lazy.

The Asians: Short. Slanty eyed. Eat rice. Eat more rice. Eat dogs, with rice. Good only for doing laundry and nails and laying rails. Devious: Work hard to make us look bad, but are actually lazy.

The Africans: Live in the jungle. Make strange clicking noise that they call language. Tried to kill Tarzan, Jane and Boy. Stole name of their country from Toto song. Lazy.

The Germans: Drunken, beer-swilling kraut-eaters. Vocabulary limited to "Ach!" and "Du Lieber!" Live in chalets. Wear funny hats and suspenders with shorts. Lazy.

The Russians: Eat borscht. Drink vodka. Women athletes look like men. Men are either soldiers or ballet dancers. Hate James Bond. Lazy.

The French: Drunken, promiscuous frog-eaters. Mimes. Think they can sing, but can't. Mispronounce "Notre Dame." Love Jerry Lewis. Wear striped shirts and berets. Lazy.

The Gays: Look funny. Walk funny. Talk funny. Dress funny. Smell good. Support same-sex marriage because serial monogamists are not destroying the institution of marriage fast enough. Cook, sew and decorate really well. Lazy.

The Blacks: Kinky hair. Smelly. Hung like mules (bucks). Big butts (wenches). Like waddymelons. Lazy.

The Dames: Weak. Scheming. Mouthy. Bitchy. Catty. Use sex as a weapon. Emotional. Useless once a month. Take men's jobs but can't handle them. Lazy unless men keep them in line.

The Columnists: Have "opinions." Use words that people have to look up. Use two words when one word will do. Write sentences so long that readers lose track of where they are, and then ... um, where was I? ... allow column to veer off course until it is brought back on track by an editor who couldn't write, so became an editor and ... SQUIRREL!!! Lazy. Except at deadline.

Essays

Two longer pieces follow. "Childhood's End" is an expanded version of an essay I submitted to a college class called, oddly enough, "Writing the Essay." My professor liked it and asked, "Have you thought about publishing?" So I did. For 40 years. It appears in print here for the first time.

The second piece was first published in 2014 in *Dead Center Magazine* (DCM) for the 50th anniversary of the Beatles' appearance on "The Ed Sullivan Show." DCM is the brainchild and obsession of my longtime friend Dave "Fig" Higgins. A playwright/editor/publisher/drummer, Fig played in many a band with me and has been a constant source of amusement for more than 40 years. I fondly recall the night I met him in 1973, when he ate all my Tic Tacs. But that is a tale for another collection. Fig claims that I am the best columnist in the United States. I tell him he needs to read more.

DM

Childhood's End

Author's note: Pressed to it, I imagine most of us could pick a single moment when, despite our being too young to realize it, adulthood began. For some of us, in involves an earth-shaking event like the death of a parent, or finding out your girlfriend is pregnant, or getting drafted. Mine was not of this caliber, but it marks — at least in my mind — the beginning of my independence. After the events that follow unfolded, I never again had to answer to my parents.

My heart is pounding as I step out of Randy's '50 Ford. The gravel in the alley crunches as I walk toward my house. I'm 18. It's nearly 1 o'clock on a Monday morning. But inside the house, it's high noon. Because I'm headed for a showdown.

I turn the key in the back door's deadbolt and step inside. The house is dark except for the glow of the 15-watt nightlight in the kitchen. I close the door softly. It won't matter; he'll hear me. I make it through the kitchen and into the dining room before I sense his presence.

"And where have you been, mister?"

Mister: His angry name for me for as long as I can remember.

He flips on the overhead light. He's not wearing his glasses, which makes the heavy bags under his eyes stand out more than if they were hidden behind his horn-rimmed bifocals. He's 57 but looks older, even though his hair is still witch's-cat black. His thin legs dangle like strings from his boxer shorts, his sleeveless undershirt reveals the "farmer's tan" that stops just where the short sleeves of his work shirt end. A high school dropout, he has worked outdoors most of his life.

"Out lookin' for jobs," I say.

It's only a partial lie. I've been out with Randy, a guitar player friend, but we hadn't really been looking for a job for our band.

Dad & me, 1956.

We've been at a bar in West Virginia, where 18-year-olds can legally sample the nectar of 3.2 beer. I'd never had any kind of beer. But Randy ordered one, so I did, too. I didn't like the taste. It's probably still sitting, unfinished, on our postage-stamp-size table.

That I've been drinking is not the problem. That I've been in a bar is not the problem. That tomorrow is a school day and it's after midnight is not the problem.

That I'd gone out on a Sunday is the problem. Because Sunday, as my parents have told me every week since I first developed the urge to play stickball with my friends after church—is a Day of Rest, ordained by God himself. On Sunday, no unnecessary activities are permitted. No excessive noise is permitted. And, definitely, going out to a bar and drinking and coming home after midnight are not permitted. God would not be happy. Neither is he.

"You think you're pretty smart, don't you?" he says. "Sneaking out when I'm at church!"

"I didn't sneak out!" I counter. "Mom said it was OK."

"Humph! I make the rules, not your mother. As long as you live in my house you'll live by my rules. You think you can pull the wool over my eyes. Going out with those freaks. You'll never get anywhere with this … music!"

I've memorized this speech. He delivers it the same each time—walking away, turned half from me, his left shoulder dipped slightly, never looking at me until he turns at the end of each sentence. And each time I hear it, I react the same behind his back. I sneer, lift my right arm, the back of my hand toward him, and pull my arm back as if to slap him. I'm safe doing this. He never turns toward me in mid-sentence. Except for tonight. He turns. His eyes widen, his neck reddens.

"Don't you raise your hand to me, mister!" He is livid, but the dining room table between us prevents him from moving toward me. "I've had enough of your monkeyshines!" he spits out, wagging his finger. "If you don't like it here, you can leave."

He shakes his head. Then, apparently wishing to appear benevolent, says, "Now get a sandwich and a glass of milk and go to bed."

"I'm not hungry," I say, my cheeks burning. I *am* hungry. But he will not dictate my eating habits.

"Then get upstairs."

I hang my jacket on the back of a chair and stomp the 13 steps up to my room, muttering, and snap on the light.

"I don't have to put up with this shit!" I say, now out of earshot. "I've had enough of this shit. I can't take any more of this … shit!" No stranger to expletives, I somehow can't find another. Still fuming, I pull his old brown suitcase from my closet and start to fill it with socks and underwear. Apparently, I'm leaving.

The linoleum floor under me is squeaking. Oh, shit! He knows I'm not in bed yet! Immediately, I hear him ascending the stairs. Panicked, I turn off my bedroom light—the switch is in the hallway outside my room—and shut the door. If the room is dark, he'll just go away, I think. I am very stupid.

The light comes on. Damn! He knows where the switch is! The door flies open. He spots the suitcase, open on my bed.

"And just what do you think you're doing, mister?"

He has called my bluff.

"I'm ... I'm leaving!"

I have no idea where I'll go.

"Good!" he shouts. "Leave! See if I care. Support yourself. You'll never make any money with music. What do you think I do all day, sit on my rear end and play?"

"Barney!" A voice from the hallway.

Mom has heard everything and followed us upstairs. She's barefoot, wearing her white silk nightgown. She looks exactly like what she is: a naive Iowa girl born in 1912.

"I suppose now you'll go and defend him," he says. He shoves past Mom and stomps down the stairs.

"What are you doing?" Mom asks.

"I'm leaving!" I continue to throw socks and underwear into the suitcase. Somehow, pants and shirts don't seem necessary.

"Oh, don't be silly!" she says. "Where will you go?"

"Somewhere," I say. "I'll go to Jim's house. I can't take any more of this ... stuff." I never swear in front of my parents.

"Oh, David, you know how he is. ... He doesn't mean it. Your father forgets when he was young."

"No," I say. "I'm leaving."

She stands, hands on hips, and heaves a sigh. "Please don't go."

I look up. "I have to."

"Stay ..." she pleads. "Do it for me."

She almost has me there. But I am a rock. I am steely in my self-righteousness. I am staunch as the Union line at Gettysburg.

"No," I say, and walk out of the room, her trailing behind. I'm halfway down the steps when her words stop me in my tracks.

"Wait ... I'll drive you."

I'm flabbergasted. Mom is helping me run away.

* * *

I stand in the dining room as she disappears into their bedroom, then emerges, dressed, and takes her coat out of the hall closet. He is sitting, smoking a Chesterfield, in the rocking chair she bought him for Christmas five years ago. He says nothing.

Mom puts her coat on. On her feet are the lace-up white nurse's shoes she wears to ease her arthritis. Her purse is over her left arm, keys to our Rambler in her right hand. We go out the kitchen door, our shoes scattering the gravel as we reach the car.

"Where are we going?" I ask as she slams the driver's door.

"To Pat's," Mom says. Pat is my sister, 12 years older than I. She moved out when I was 9 to get away from him.

During the drive, Mom attempts to reason with me.

"You father means well," she says. She adjusts the rearview mirror. She says it was worse for my sister and two older brothers, who grew up separated by only five years. She tells me that once, he put the three kids in the car after they'd been arguing amongst themselves, then drove them out into the country in the dead of night and through the gate of the orphanage. Then he threw open his door, pulled the back of the driver's seat forward and ordered them out. But they had cried, and he had relented.

Pat, holding Spooky. Despite my having held a gun on her here, she took me in 9 years later.

She tells me that my eldest brother joined the Air Force to get away from him. That my other brother joined the Army to get away from him. That Pat left home as soon she could because he never liked her. "Because she was a girl," she says, matter-of-fact-ly.

"And once," she says, "he paddled you so hard that it left you black and blue. That was the last time I ever let him touch you."

I don't recall that incident, but I do remember his favored punishment: spanking me with a wooden paddle that originally had a rubber ball attached via an elastic band—an instrument meant to be merrily thwack-twanged by gleeful children, not used as an torture device worthy of Torquemada.

"Your father forgets when he was young," she says again.

I sit silently. I am unmoved. I am the Spartans at Thermopylae.

Ten minutes later we arrive at Pat's. Its 2 a.m. We walk to the front door. Mom knocks. Pat's face, her eyes half closed, appears in the half-moon window. The door opens. She's holding the sawed-off baseball bat she keeps by her bed as protection against burglars. Bleary eyed, she simply stares, bewildered.

Mom explains. Pat shakes her head. "This sounds familiar."

Mom asks if Pat will allow me to stay. If she'll drive me to school in the morning. She will. Mom hugs me and says, "I'll talk to him. Stop after school tomorrow."

I bunk on Pat's couch. "You know, I left, too," she says.

"I see that. And mom told me about the orphanage thing"

"But not about everything. Goodnight."

*　　*　　*

Pat drives me to school in the morning. I tell my three best friends that I've left home. They rally round, tell me I've done the right thing. Jim tells me he can't let me stay with him, but I can sleep under a nearby bridge—he has a sleeping bag. I leave school, a modern-day Israelite, wandering.

I stop at home, as Mom requested. The house is quiet, yet I know he's not at work because the Rambler is parked in the alley.

Inside, Mom is alone in the dining room, doing a crossword puzzle. She says he is upstairs in the spare bedroom. He's probably reading the religious pamphlets he ordered from the Billy Graham Crusade. Or perhaps he is reading his King James Bible, the one in which he has underlined in red ink his favorite passages:

Honour thy father and thy mother: that thy days may be long upon the land which the LORD thy God giveth thee.

A foolish son is the calamity of his father: and the contentions of a wife are a continual dropping.

Mom tells me she has arranged for me to stay with my paternal grandmother "for a few days." His mother! Insult added to injury. I am delighted. Mom goes upstairs to my room and returns with pants and shirts, then drives me to Grandma's, five blocks away. On the way, she tries to explain what happened the night before.

She tells me that he dropped out of school when he was 16. The year before, his father had died of a stroke. My grandmother, having lost her left leg to cancer, couldn't work. "He worked in the brickyard," Mom says. "Grandma took all his money."

"He had it hard," she continues. "Your father forgets when he was young."

I want to say, no ... he remembers exactly what it was like when he was young. And he's taking it out on me. But I merely listen.

Mom accompanies me into Grandma's, takes me in, gets me settled.

"I'll see you," she says. Then she's gone.

Grandma shows me the room I'll be sleeping in. Thankfully, it's not the room in which she keeps her artificial leg, which she refuses to wear—the room I'm still afraid to enter because, when I was 8, Grandma sent me into it to retrieve a Thanksgiving pumpkin pie. The prosthesis, leaning in the corner near the dessert, had so terrified me that I'd returned, pieless.

But I'm happy at Grandma's. She never tells when to be home or what to do. When I get home at 3 a.m. on a school night after playing in a bar with my band, she isn't waiting for me. But a salami sandwich and a glass of milk are. Yeah, I like my new home.

* * *

Three weeks pass. I have stopped to see Mom on my walk from school several times. I stop again. The Rambler is again parked outside.

Seated at the dining room table, Mom looks up.

"He wants you to come home," she says. "He says he will never bother you or tell you what to do again. He says he's sorry."

I know she's lying: he has said nothing.

I am steely in my self-righteousness. I am the R.A.F. during the Battle of Britain.

"OK," I say.

"Good," Mom says. "I'll get my car keys." She disappears into their bedroom.

Yes, I'll come home. He has learned his lesson.

And all my clothes are dirty.

In My Life

How the Beatles Saved Me, and Everyone

Author's note: Some incidents have been combined, but they all occurred. Names have not been changed. I trust my friends will forgive me.

It hung there in the window of the Brighton Music Center, the candy-apple-red culmination of all my teenage hopes and dreams: a shiny new Kingston electric bass. All that stood between it and my becoming a rock star was a sheet of plate glass. And $99.95.

I'd walked by that window every Tuesday for nearly two years going to and from my trombone lessons, never stopping. But something that happened two days earlier made me acutely aware of this long-necked, seductive thing of beauty. That something occurred on Sunday, February 9, 1964. Like most

1965: Hair just starting to grow

American families of the Cold War era, mine observed the Sunday tradition of watching "The Ed Sullivan Show" at 8 p.m. That night I saw the Beatles for the first time, as did an estimated 74 million Americans. I expected them to be great. But I didn't expect to fall in love with Paul McCartney.

Love may seem too strong a word to use in describing what happened that night. But it isn't. When the Beatles' bassist turned to Ringo Starr and counted off "All My Loving," then stepped to the microphone and began to sing, I knew he was singing for me. Only me. It was a religious epiphany that I have never again experienced. Two minutes and 13 seconds later, I knew I was meant to play bass. I also knew I had little chance of weaseling a hundred bucks out of my parents.

I couldn't approach my father, who worked a $1.25-per-hour minimum wage job as a gas station attendant. Two years previously he'd refused to pay $50 for a trombone so I could join the junior high school band. My brother Harry, who played trombone and upright bass in a big band, had sprung for that. But Mom ... at least she would listen to my spiel. "That's a lot of money," Mom said. "We'll see." I knew that phrase. It meant "no."

*　*　*

Despite having no instruments, several of my friends and I became proto-Beatles. First we let our crewcuts grow out so our bangs could slash across our foreheads at a 45-degree angle. Then we pegged the legs of our black pants and topped them with black turtleneck sweaters. Finally we bought black Thom McAn Cuban-heeled Beatle boots, installed metal cleats on their heels, and went clacking down the slate-floored corridors of our high school, occasionally careening out of control when the worn-down cleats caused our feet to slip out from under us. Yeah, we were cool.

By late 1964, we were ready to form a band. Denny's widowed father bought a set of drums for him, wisely knowing they would keep his son off the streets. Denny thought we could recruit Tom, who had a very cool Silvertone guitar with an amplifier built into its case. But Tom proved to be more interested in his Honda 50 motor scooter. So we approached Jim. Jim was a local legend—he had not only a guitar with a separate amplifier, but also a father who had let him grow his hair over his ears and into pudding-basin bangs. Finally, we recruited Mike, a bassist who agreed to play guitar so I could play bass.

Only problem was, I still didn't have a bass. Undaunted, early in 1965 I began practicing on my brother's upright. That I was able to reproduce McCartney's bass lines by listening to "The Beatles Second Album" reinforced my conviction that Paul had passed his powers to me through the TV tube almost a year earlier.

When I returned home after school one afternoon in May 1965, a complete bass guitar outfit was waiting for me in the dining room. Mom had purchased it from the Spiegel's catalog using money she'd inherited from her father's estate. She hadn't told me she was doing so, nor had she told Dad; he didn't think being a musician was a real career option.

Our instrumentation now complete, we were ready to rock. Look out, Beatles—the Sting Rays are coming!

*   *   *

Although the Summer of Love didn't bloom until 1967, Denny, Jim, Mike and I planted its seeds in the summer of '65. We set up our equipment in Denny's basement and rehearsed almost every day after school let out in late May. Within three weeks we had learned 50 songs by the Beatles, the Animals, the Searchers, the Rolling Stones, the Zombies and many more British Invasion groups. Neighborhood girls flocked to Denny's house, sitting on the basement steps, screaming and applauding after every number. Because the Dave Clark Five had a sax player, we thought it a cool idea to recruit Frank, from nearby Beaver Falls, to play tenor.

June 1965: The Sting Rays play the Saturday night canteen dance. Girls and boys alike crowd against us on the gym floor, enthralled by the sight of a *real, live band*. After the dance, I allow several girls to sign my arm in purple ink, not realizing that it is I who should be signing their arms. My girlfriend is not happy.

No one notices that Palma, Denny's girlfriend, has spent most of the night standing near Jim. We all know Palma. When she feels that Denny is spending too much time with the group, Palma climbs to the top of a war monument in the park next door to Denny's house, pretends to be stuck and asks for help to get down, all the while knowing we are staring up at her foam-covered breasts under her loose-fitting shirt.

July 1965: Jim is late for practice. Finally, his Beatle boots appear at the top of Denny's stairs, but do not descend.

"Dave?" Jim's voice says softly. "C'mere."

I climb the steps and meet him on the side porch.

"You're late," I say, the leader of the band.

"I quit," says Jim, no longer a member of the band.

I am momentarily speechless.

"It's Palma," he says. "I love her, but she loves Denny. I can't be in the band with her around."

What can I do? I love Denny, too. A week later Terry, a guitarist Frank knows, takes Jim's place. Bob—Terry and Frank's bass-player friend—comes along. To watch, Bob says.

August 1965: The Sting Rays play at a wedding reception for a friend's sister. We charge $35. At the end of the reception, the bride's father approaches me and says, "How 'bout I give you 20 bucks and some gum?"

I refuse. The Beatles do not play for gum. Nor will we.

September 1965: Summer vacation ends. A rock band consisting of 16-year-olds can't play in bars, where bands can make as much as $75 a night, so we must be content to play at school dances. But gigs there have been few and far between, mostly because the Surfers, the other band from our town, is better than us in both the music and looks departments. Still, we rehearse every week.

January 1966: The Sting Rays, fresh from a New Year's Eve gig at the Conway Croation Club, have scheduled a rehearsal. I descend the stairs to Denny's basement. When I reach the bottom, Bob—he who supposedly only watches—is standing in my place, his bass in hand, his expensive Vox bass amp behind him.

Before I can speak, Denny says, "We're quitting."

Confused, I say, "You mean I'm fired?"

No, Denny says, his cheeks flushed. "We're joining Bob."

I'm more confused. Should I be proud that in the history of music, I may be the only bass player whose band quit him rather than fire him? But my 16-year-old temper prevails.

"You're quitting? Well, I'll show you! I'm taking my stuff! All my stuff! I paid for these wires! I'm taking them!"

And I do, even though the wires are soldered to the backs of the speakers we use for a public address system. I rip them off and stuff them into a pocket.

"You'll pay for this!" Mike says.

I grab my amp and climb the stairs in silence, then use Denny's phone to call Mom.

Denny follows me to the kitchen. "What can we do?" he says apologetically. "Bob can get us jobs at Conneaut Lake Park." I ignore him.

Ten minutes later, Mom arrives.

"What happened?" Mom asks.

"They quit me!" I respond.

"Well, David," she says, "there's plenty of fish in the sea."

And she is right.

* * *

When I stopped counting in the 1980s, I had played in something like 20 rock bands. The Sting Rays broke up before the summer of 1966. Denny and I played in two more bands together before I left town in 1970. We are Facebook friends but I haven't seen him since 1975. Terry and I played in one more band together; he died of a heart attack in his mid-40s. Jim got over Palma; I found him on Facebook, but he died before we could re-connect. Mike is also a Facebook friend. I still haven't "paid for this."

Fifty-one years later, I'm still playing bass. Fifty-one years later, I'm still that 14-year-old whose life changed forever on February 9, 1964.

*　　*　　*

It's difficult today to explain to anyone younger than 40 exactly how four "Lads from Liverpool" could have had such an effect on millions of lives, to drive home just how much power music had in 1964—the power to change, to enhance, to justify life.

Today we live in an era of downloadable, throwaway music that serves as little more than the soundtrack for texting while walking. Rock stars are famous not for writing and singing great songs, but for twerking in their underwear.

The Beatles had style, humor, *savoir faire*. The Beatles rewrote the rules—not only of music, but of life itself. They changed forever the viable ways for young men and women to make a living. And not only that.

The Beatles were the light at the end of the pitch-black tunnel leading out of the JFK assassination, and they arrived just in time that cold February night. Life, so rife with possibilities just two months earlier, seemed to have been drained of vigor, of possibilities. Even music—meant to alleviate just such hopelessness—had as the number one song for the first four weeks of 1964 Bobby Vinton's insipid "There, I've Said It Again."

The Beatles changed all that. They saved music. They saved a whole generation by giving it a voice and a focus. The anti-war movement, the civil rights movement, the women's movement: all stepped to the beat of "All You Need Is Love."

The Beatles saved me. They saved everyone.

About the Author

Dave Molter grew up in New Brighton, Pennsylvania, about 35 miles northwest of Pittsburgh. There he lived a rather normal childhood and planned to become an English teacher. But at 15 he discovered the Beatles, and everything changed. After teaching himself to play bass guitar, he joined a series of rock bands, slipped the surly bonds of the Beaver Valley and took up residence in the suburbs of the nearest large city that begins with a "P." There he lurked, disguised as, variously, a musician, writer, editor, retail manager and communications wage slave.

He is a two-time winner of the Pennsylvania Newspaper Publishers Association *Keystone Press Award* for columns and was nominated for Pittsburgh's *Golden Quill Awards.* Dave freelances today by writing a biweekly humor column for the Washington (Pa.) *Observer-Reporter* newspaper and as a contributing writer for *Dead Center Magazine*, a quarterly arts publication based in State College, Pennsylvania. He still wants to be a Beatle.

About the Illustrator

Graphic designer and illustrator **Michael J. Andrulonis** triumphed over profound trauma to become an award-winning artist. He spent his early childhood with a bath towel pinned to his T-shirt; in despair when he learned that he was not a super hero, he turned to art for consolation. His fascination with fantasy worlds helped him develop a distinctive cartooning style that has enlivened healthcare, retail, technology, and nonprofit projects as well as dozens of books and other publications. A Pittsburgh resident, Andrulonis still occasionally dons a pair of spangled tights and prowls local parking lots, looking for shoppers who fail to return carts. Learn more about Michael at www.andrudesign.com.

Made in the USA
Lexington, KY
02 September 2017